D0194275

Jonathan Chesner

free spirit
PUBLISHING®

Library of Congress Cataloging-in-Publication Data
Chesner, Jonathan.
  ADHD in HD: brains gone wild / by Jonathan Chesner.
    p. cm.
  ISBN 978-1-57542-386-9 (pbk.)
  1. Attention-deficit disorder in adolescence. 2. Anxiety in adolescence. 3. Teenagers—Family relationships. I. Title.
  RJ506.H9C476 2012
  618.92'8589—dc23

                                                                    2011047036
eBook ISBN: 978-1-57542-671-6

Free Spirit Publishing does not have control over or assume responsibility for author or third-party websites and their content. At the time of this book's publication, all facts and figures cited within are the most current available. All telephone numbers, addresses, and website URLs are accurate and active; all publications, organizations, websites, and other resources exist as described in this book; and all have been verified as of November 2011. If you find an error or believe that a resource listed here is not as described, please contact Free Spirit Publishing. Parents, teachers, and other adults: We strongly urge you to monitor children's use of the Internet.

The concepts, ideas, and suggestions contained in this book are not intended as substitutes for professional healthcare.

Reading Level Grades 7 & Up; Interest Level Ages 13 & Up; Fountas & Pinnell Guided Reading Level Z

Edited by Eric Braun
Cover, interior design, and illustrations by Tasha Kenyon

10 9 8 7 6 5 4 3 2 1
Printed in the United States of America
B10950212

Free Spirit Publishing Inc.
Minneapolis, MN
(612) 338-2068
help4kids@freespirit.com
www.freespirit.com

Free Spirit offers competitive pricing.
Contact edsales@freespirit.com for pricing information on multiple quantity purchases.

I'd like to dedicate this to two awesome dogs, Keisha and Bear (RIP).

Oh, and to all the special brains out there.

Okay, so I'd like to dedicate this to Keisha, Bear, and special brains.

Oops, and my buddy Steve Nusinow.

So dogs, special brains, and Steve . . . final answer.

 —JC

CONTENTS

TOPIC KEY

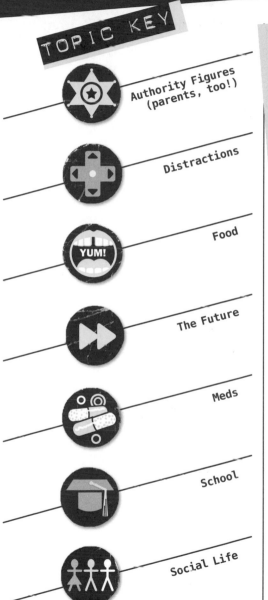

Authority Figures (parents, too!)

Distractions

Food

The Future

Meds

School

Social Life

Foreword
(by Jeffrey Rowe, M.D.)...... ix

Melting Your Face Off with the Flames of Awesomeness
(introduction to the book).... 1

ME DOLPHIN/YOU ELEPHANT / 6

(the day I realized I was a lot more hyper than other kids)

MY TURN / 8

(talking & listening, the difference)

DISGUISES / 10

(behaving well in potentially hostile territory)

HI, I'M A SPECIAL BRAIN / 12

(dealing with ill-informed people)

SIX WORDS THAT GO GREAT TOGETHER / 14

(sticking up for personal decisions)

IT WASN'T ME, IT WAS A-D-D! / 16

(what to expect when diagnosed)

KEEPING IT REAL / 18

(when to speak up and
when to put a lid
on it)

**KEEP IT DOWN . . . HEY,
WHAT'S UP?** / 20

(silence: a love/hate
relationship)

THE 7:30 TO 3:30 / 22

(yearning for
learning not to
feel so burning)

THE CLASS-ICKS / 24

(what to do about
classes that make
you go "ick")

COMIC BOOK CLASS / 26

(asking for alterna-
tive assignments)

**YEAH, THAT'S GOING
TO BE A PROBLEM** / 28

(after-class burnout)

**TAKING A TEST AT THE SPEED
OF A TUMBLEWEED** / 30

(not being able to
finish stuff)

SQUARE PEG, ROUND HOLE / 32

(finding the best way
to learn)

**TELL ME WHAT YOU WANT
(WHATCHA REALLY, REALLY
WANT)** / 34

(getting the who/what/
where explained to you
right the first time)

SUBJECTS OF DEATH / 36

(more about tough
classes)

**A POSITIVE PERSPECTIVE
ON SCHOOL** / 40

('cause it's too easy
to look at the glass
as half empty)

TV / 42

(television and you)

BRAIN PEP TALK / 44

(isolating negative
things and staying
positive)

FREAKING OUT / 46

(learning not to worry
about failure)

JOBS / 48

(doing anything
you want)

WHY RULES EXIST / 50

(the day I learned why
rules exist)

HOLD THE FERN / 52

(dealing with
distracting things)

DREAMLAND / 54

(when your imagination
gets out of control
and you zone off)

THE DOC / 56

(getting meds from the
psychiatrist)

LOOKING AROUND / 58

 (easily distracted or overly observant?)

RADNESS! / 60

 (getting excited on random stuff)

CLASS: BUCKLE UP, IT MIGHT GET BUMPY / 62

 (picking the best seat in the classroom)

RIGHT WHEN I START GETTING GOOD / 64

 (getting left behind while trying to follow along)

FADE TO CHINESE / 66

 (difficulty with learning for more than one hour at a time)

READY, SET, DONE / 68

 (finishing things too quickly)

FOOT TAPPING FOR HEALTH AND WELLNESS / 70

 (fidgeting your way to more defined calf muscles)

MAKING FRIENDS IN THE OFFICE / 72

 (finding new friends in unlikely places)

OLD PEOPLE / 74

 (really wise people with good advice)

GIRLS (OR GUYS) / 76

 (plenty of fish in the sea)

NO, REALLY? / 78

 (famous special brains)

GIRLS (OR GUYS) PART 2 / 80

 (hotness isn't everything)

BULLY BEING BULLY / 82

 (bullies, bullying, and other bull)

OLD LADIES AND INAPPROPRIATE HANDSHAKES DON'T MIX / 86

 (saying the wrong thing to the wrong person)

SOCIAL MEDIA FOR DUMMIES / 88

 (being a responsible Internet citizen)

SELECTIVE HEARING / 90

 (tuning out)

GOOD POINT / 92

 (focusing on your strengths)

VICTORIES / 94

 (turning your A in PE or computer class into a life mantra)

TEAM EXPLORE / 96

 (finding out how you learn best)

PUTTING AN ASSIGNMENT ON PAYMENT PLANS / 98

(procrastinating)

BREAK IT DOWN / 100

(not getting overwhelmed when you have a full plate)

LAZY? / 104

(the difference between lazy and bored)

WORRYING / 106

(how to do less of it)

COULD HAVE BEEN A MILLIONAIRE TIME #113 / 108

(following through on good ideas)

FUTURE EMPLOYMENT? / 110

(uninvented jobs that I think would be cool)

A FEW REAL-WORLD PEOPLE YOU SHOULD KNOW ABOUT / 112

(they did some pretty inspiring things)

VIDEO GAMES VS. A SLAP IN THE FACE FROM REALITY / 116

(making the most out of every situation)

THE BAD DAY VS. A SLAP IN THE FACE FROM REALITY / 118

(why bad days often aren't as bad as they seem)

WE ONLY EAT WITH FREE-RANGE FORKS / 120

(eating a commonsense diet)

SNACK TIME / 122

(food advice)

A LETTER TO MY EX-LOVER, CANDY / 126

(avoiding too many sweets)

JUDGE, JURY, AND EXECUTIONER / 128

(you may have inherited your special brain from a family member—use that to your advantage)

TIME OUT! / 130

(a strategy for when things get heated)

FOLLOWING YOUR HEART / 132

(what to do at a fork in the road)

BIG DREAMS / 136

(why you should pursue big things)

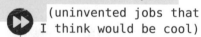

Glossary 138

Index 140

Acknowledgments 144

About the Author 145

Foreword

I'm so glad Jonathan Chesner wrote this book, and I'll tell you why.

I have been a psychiatrist for 26 years, and a child and adolescent psychiatrist for 20 of those years. I have worked in a variety of places with a variety of people—everyone from little kids with autism to bigger kids with anger management problems who were in juvenile hall. I give more than 50 lectures a year about mental health problems, family troubles, the impact of trauma on young children, and ADHD, the subject of this book.

And yet, the more I learn and teach others about mental health problems, the more I realize how little I really know. And *that's* why I'm so glad Jonathan wrote this book. Mental health problems such as ADHD are common among school-age children. But funny, informative books about mental health problems are not so common.

This book gives me—and more importantly you—a rare and awesome window into real knowledge about ADHD: what it means and how it feels. How to cope with it and succeed with it. That's because Jonathan *has* ADHD. He has coped with it, and he has succeeded with it. In this book he shares some of the secrets about how his brain works, thinks, feels, and solves problems. I learn something new each time I read it, and I know you will, too.

And this is important: I also laugh so hard each time I read it that it brings tears to my eyes.

I've worked with Jonathan as his psychiatrist since he was a young teenager. When he first came to me about his ADHD, he didn't talk much. He wasn't terrifically happy to see me, and there were times when I didn't think our treatment relationship would survive. He didn't always like what I said, and he had interesting ways of getting that across to me, like trying to throw a chair through my window three times during one session. But he always came back for help because he knew things weren't going well.

He talks to me now, by the way. Now I can't get the guy to shut up.

Chances are, if you're holding this book in your hands, you have ADHD as well. And I'm guessing—and Jonathan and I are both hoping—that you will relate to many of the stories Jonathan shares about his journey through ADHD. You'll learn about treatment and how your brain works—it's actually pretty cool—and how you can use your ADHD for you, not against you, in school, at home, and with your friends.

ADHD in HD: Brains Gone Wild is meant to be read quickly, and over and over. You'll probably wear out your copy before you know it, because unlike other books about ADHD, this book is especially for you—not parents, teachers, doctors, or anyone else. And it's the only book on ADHD infused with Jonathan's funny, fresh, bold, and honest perspective. He doesn't sugarcoat his experiences, and he offers practical advice and solutions to problems you have likely faced yourself.

Get ready to have fun.

—Jeffrey Rowe, M.D.

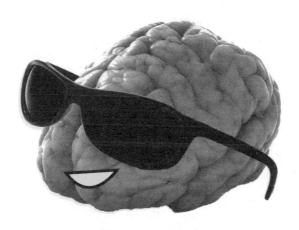

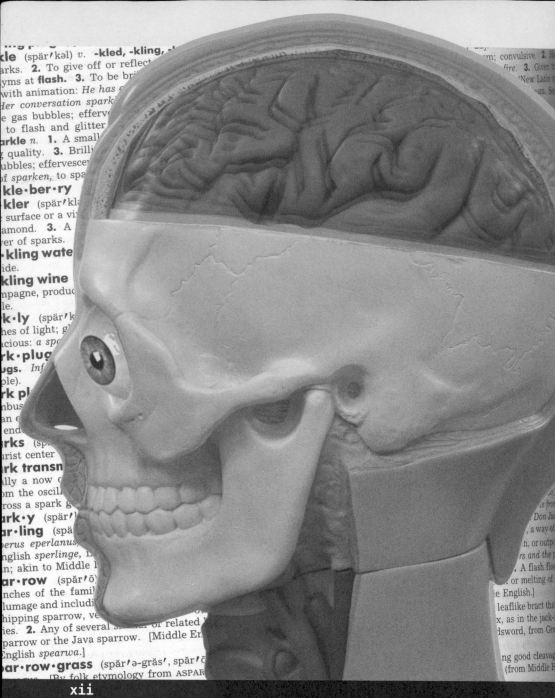

Special Brain: A type of brain that has an overactive thought pattern and/or difficulty sitting still. Although often highly intelligent, special brains have trouble focusing on things that seem mundane or difficult. They often lack inhibition and express whatever is on their mind or in their heart. Many are diagnosed with the condition attention deficit disorder (ADD) or attention deficit hyperactivity disorder (ADHD).

---

to; engender. *tyraming ….* ; bring forth; produce: *a family that had spawned* To plant with mycelia grown in specially prepared r. [Middle English *spawne*, from *spawnen*, to Anglo-Norman *espaundre*, from Latin *expandere*. **—spawn′er** *n.*

v. **spayed, spay·ing, spays.** To remove surgi- ies of (an animal). [Middle English *spaien*, from n espeier, to cut with a sword, from *espee. sword* atha. See SPA

ociety for the ciety for the

spoke *tr.* **1.** To nodulatic ns orally ey are n e: *The p* e a stater **b.** To ac vey a m *words.* ealing: *Hi* or reque ce for the l und: *The dr* guns or ca give an indi d upbringing. — e words of wisdo (a language): *spe* the truth. **b.** To express in writing. **4.** *Nautical.* To mmunicate with (another vessel) at sea. **5.** To convey al means: *His eyes spoke volumes.* **—phrasal verbs.** t. To talk freely and fearlessly, as about a public issue. , **1.** To speak loud enough to be audible. **2.** To speak ar or hesitation. **—idioms. so to speak.** In a manner g. *can't see the forest for the trees, so to speak.* **speak** To speak condescendingly to: *She never spoke down to* ence. **to speak of.** Worthy of mention: *There's nothing* eak of. [Middle English *speken*, from Old English *spre-* on.] **—speak′a·ble** *adj.*

YMS: *speak, talk, converse, discourse.* These verbs mean s one's thoughts by uttering words. *Speak* and *talk*, often ngeable, are the most general: *He ate his meal without* aking to his dinner companion. *"Why don't you speak for* John?" (Henry Wadsworth Longfellow). *"On an occasion* ind *it becomes more than a moral duty to speak one's* It *becomes a pleasure"* (Oscar Wilde). *I want to talk with* out *vacation plans.* *"We must know . . . what we are talking* Henry James). *"Let's talk sense to the American people"* ….ses interchange of thoughts

of two large marine game fishes (*Tetrapturus …* *belone*) related to the sailfish and marlin, having the up elongated into a spearlike projection.

spear·fish² (spîr′fĭsh′) *intr.v.* **-fished, -fish·ing, -** To fish with a spear, spearlike implement, or spe **—spear′fish′er** *n.* **—spear′fish′ing** *n.*

spear grass *n.* See **feather grass.**

ooting a

d head of . The driv **—spearh** er of: *"sp* uses [and)

y a soldie

asian pl wers an

several ammula flower ications **pec** *tr.t* To wr ating to constru

…, *a spec job; a s* **—idiom. on spec.** On a speculation basis; with no as profit: *houses built on spec; writes TV commercial* **—spec′′er** *n.*

spec. *abbr.* **1.** Special. **2.** Specifically. **3.** Specifi Speculation.

spe·cial (spĕsh′əl) *adj. Abbr.* **sp., spec. 1.** Surpass common or usual; exceptional: *a special occasion; a sp* **2. a.** Distinct among others of a kind: *a special type* special medication for arthritis. **b.** Primary: *His spec* tion comes from volunteer work. **3.** Peculiar to a spe or thing; particular: *my own special chair; the specia* a computer. **4. a.** Having a limited or specific functi tion, or scope: *a special role in the mission.* **b.** Arr particular occasion or purpose: *a special visit from h* **5.** Regarded with particular affection and admiratio friend. **6.** Additional; extra: *a special holiday flight.* **1.** Something arranged, issued, or appropriated to service or occasion: *rode to work on the commuter sp* featured attraction, such as a reduced price: *a specia* **3.** A single television production that features a spe given topic, or a particular performer. [Middle Englis French *especial*, from Latin *speciālis*, from *speciēs*, k ….al·ly adv. **spe′cial·ness** *n.*

Melting Your Face Off with the Flames of Awesomeness

Greetings, and thanks for picking up this book.

You holding this in your hands means one of several things:

1) You have incredible taste in literature and decided you needed something that would impress people when they saw it on your desk.

2) You have a special brain and wanted to buy the best book ever written on the subject.

3) Someone else saw this, bought it, and left it sitting on your bed with a note saying "Read me."

4) Your TV stand is off-center and this book is the perfect size to make it straight.

Whatever the reason, thanks for picking up *ADHD in HD*. Making this book has been a dream come true for me. A lot of people throw out the phrase "dream come true," but I really mean it. I really struggled with some parts of growing up (both the school and social stuff), and I always knew that if I figured out how to make my life easier, I would share it with other people like me. Not only would I share it, I would present it in a way that I would want to read, with pictures and funny stories. It would feel like it was written by one of your friends, and it would have good, relevant advice that you could really use.

It took me at least 10 years of making mistakes, trying hard to get along better, and learning all I could about ADHD before I figured out all the things you'll find in this book. I'm still not perfect, but I'm getting better; so maybe in another 10 years I'll have learned more things and write a sequel.

The purpose of this book is to:

○ Help you learn from my mistakes.

○ Make you laugh.

○ Make you want to give yourself a hi-five in the mirror and say, "Special brains rule!"

Who This Book Is For: Before this book went to print, word got out that I was working on an ADHD book that would slay all other books. At first I only showed it to other people who had ADHD, but, eventually, my non-ADHD friends got hold of it as well. The non-ADHD friends really enjoyed the book, too, and, feeling generous, I tried to make it accessible to everyone. It's meant for teenagers and adults, scrawny seventh graders and chubby grandmas, and everyone in between.

Make no mistake, this is an ADHD book at its core . . . but even if you don't have ADHD, you'll find something in here worth a gander. Most importantly: reading this will give you an inside look at what it's like having a brain that won't sit still, which is helpful if you have a lot of encounters with our kind.

 How to Read This Book: You can read it however you'd like—cover-to-cover, pick and choose, upside down, or even just look at the pictures. Check out the Contents pages and you'll see that every chapter is summarized and coded with an icon so you can see what that chapter is about. It's like getting a variety pack of jelly beans but not having to dig through the whole container trying to find those elusive spotted green ones! Just flip to the flavor you want. (Spotted green = pear flavor, FYI!)

I hope a lot of what's in here will resonate with you. I know I'm not the only person who's been turned down on a date, gotten a bad grade, or said something inappropriate without thinking. If a section doesn't seem relevant to you now, maybe in a few years you'll reread it and find it useful. Some of the chapters are just for fun, but most have practical advice. All the advice is for your benefit, not to make parents happy or sell more copies. I think my advice is pretty legit, but like anything, you can take it or leave it.

Please Note: Certain parts of this book contain stuff that is specific for special brains that have ADHD. This book is not meant to offer any type of diagnosis or treatment, or be a medical authority on ADHD. There are lots of ways to manage ADHD, including (and excluding) with medicine, and I strongly suggest talking to your doctor and family about what works best for you. Taking any medicine without a prescription from a doctor is one of the most dangerous and stupid things you can do. In conclusion, don't take or do anything without your doctor's knowledge and don't try to take me to court if you do something stupid while this book is in your hands.

Who Wrote This Book: My name is Jonathan. I'm 27 years old and from San Diego, California. I was diagnosed with ADHD when I was nine years old and I haven't slowed down since. I graduated high school with a respectable GPA and decent SAT scores and attended the University of Southern California, receiving a degree in public policy.

Here are some things I've done so far:

o I've starred in television shows like *Veronica Mars, Bones, The Closer,* and *The Ex List.* I've been in commercials for Jack in the Box, Sony PlayStation, Skittles, and a bunch of other companies.

- I ran a clothing brand called NiZ Couture. I sold my stuff in several premium retailers throughout Southern California and Japan.
- I've contributed product and marketing ideas to Future Fins and Von Zipper sunglasses.
- I've traveled to far corners of the world looking for fun waves to ride and exciting creatures to observe.

I never know where my life is headed next, but I'm sure it will be an adventure.

Hi-Fives,

Jonathan Chesner

P.S. I'd be more than stoked if you want to write to me about your adventures with ADHD. You can hit me up through my publisher:

Free Spirit Publishing
217 Fifth Avenue North, Suite 200
Minneapolis, MN 55401-1299
ADHDinHD@freespirit.com

Me: *Dolphin* / You: **ELEPHANT**

I was really young when I realized that my brain wasn't like other people's brains. One way to describe it was that I had the type of brain that would wear a Hawaiian shirt, bright red pants, and cool painted shoes to a wedding. I felt like other people had brains that would wear three-piece suits and read textbooks. At school, all the other kids could sit behind their desks and be quiet, but my brain wanted to do jumping jacks in the corner.

Here's another way to put it: my brain was like a dolphin and other people's brains were like well-behaved elephants. Those brains would look at me and see some type of wild animal. But I wasn't a wild animal; I just wasn't a well-behaved elephant. And elephants can call dolphins unruly all they want, but it doesn't change the fact that dolphins are awesome!

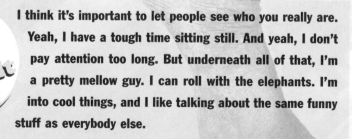

I think it's important to let people see who you really are. Yeah, I have a tough time sitting still. And yeah, I don't pay attention too long. But underneath all of that, I'm a pretty mellow guy. I can roll with the elephants. I'm into cool things, and I like talking about the same funny stuff as everybody else.

6

Finding things you share with other people is the best way to make pals. I don't care who you are, there has to be something you find interesting that others do, too (whether it's deep sea diving or reading a magazine). Even though I have never won a popularity contest, I accumulated a diverse group of friends who I could share my love of surfing, professional wrestling, and rap music with. Once other people knew that I was pretty informed and could add to the conversation, it became much easier to make friends even though they knew I sometimes had a tough time sitting still. I just needed to remember to wait my turn to talk.

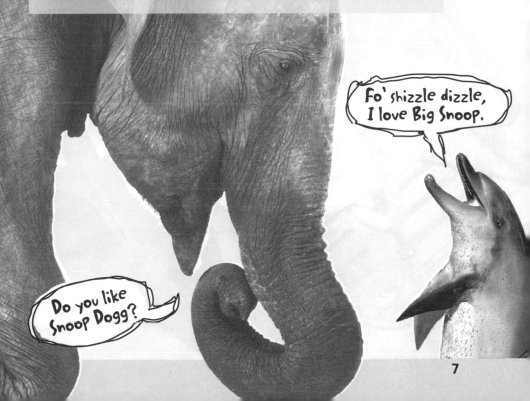

MY TURN

Whenever I'm talking with a group of people I don't know or someone I've just been introduced to, my brain gets super nervous. I'm not sure what my brain gets nervous about, and I'm working on changing it, but some types of social interactions make my heartbeat go from the speed of smooth jazz to house music.

Some people get really quiet when they get uneasy, but not me. I tend to talk a lot. Once my heart starts beating, it's inevitable that I'm going to try to steer the conversation toward what I feel comfortable talking about. (A few safe harbors for me are zoo animals, pop stars from the 1990s, and adventures.) All this talk about steering and harbors reminds me of how much fun boating is. Steering the boat is especially fun. I've been on a boat that I wasn't allowed to steer and I can tell you it was lame. Conversations are like driving a boat: people can get pretty chapped if someone is hogging the steering wheel.

King of Listening

Yo Denzel: When it comes to people I'd like to hang out with on a boat, Denzel Washington is right up there. I've seen him give interviews on TV and he looks like a great listener. He's such a great listener, he inspires me to listen just like him. I've even considered getting an H.W.D.W.L. (How Would Denzel Washington Listen?) bracelet. Denzel seems like the type of guy who has a good grasp on when to steer a conversation and when to be a passenger.

Just remember, during a conversation, sometimes you get to wear the captain's hat and sometimes you have to put on your lifejacket and be a passenger in the galley.

Disguises

Most of the time, when you're out in public or around other people, you can't be super hyper and do whatever you'd like. This is common sense, because if I did whatever I liked, I'd wear sweatpants and pee outside all day. I'm sure some people may see nothing wrong with this, but according to the local police, peeing in public is illegal. Fair or unfair, I don't want to go to jail for using my lawn as a restroom.

There are tons of things I would probably do if I didn't know they were socially unacceptable. Since special brains aren't always good at determining if something is okay or not, it can be useful to ask yourself, "Would a suit-and-tie-wearing brain do this?" A few good ways to know when it might be time to adjust your behavior is if:

a) Parents are grabbing their kids and moving to the other side of the street.

b) People come up to you and ask, "Umm . . . are you lost?"

c) Your teacher has said your name more than three times in one class period (and not in a good way).

d) People point and look at you while talking on their cell phone.

Unfortunately, the more you go out the more you're going to have to patrol your behavior. After a while, it's not that fun to constantly be asking yourself, "Should I do this? Should I do that?" A much more enjoyable way to make sure you don't create a ruckus is to imagine you are a secret agent living among non-special brains (Secret Brain 007). When you're out on a mission (like a date or something), try to stay incognito—maybe try to take the intensity level down a few decibels. (Be careful not to get amped on caffeine or sugar.)

Once you find someone who seems like they'd be pretty cool with a truer you, drop hints as to what you're like with the volume at normal (for you) levels. Since lots of non-special brains haven't dealt with people like us, gradually warm them up. You don't need to be all suit-and-tie and say, "If you please, kind sir/madam, I have ADHD" or "I'm a special brain, blah blah blah," but slowly increase the revs until your motor is running at full speed. It's like you've been wearing a trench coat and you undo a few buttons before you bust it all the way open. Then, once you feel like they're cool with you, you can drop the disguises. "Here's how I really am! Hahahahaha!" It's sort of like streaking.

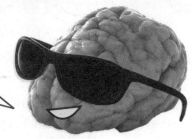

Hi, I'm a Special Brain

You know what sucks? Having to tell cynical people that you have ADHD. In my experience dealing with these types of people, one of two things happens:

1) They think ADHD is an excuse and you're just trying to get extended time on your tests or easier grading.

2) They start treating you like you're four years old.

Seriously, this rarely happens:

Person: "Why are you so squirmy? Can't you sit still and watch this?"

Me: "I'm sorry, I have ADHD and right now I really would like to go run around outside."

Person: "Oh, no worries."

My name is Jonathan, and I have a special brain. I'm not making this up, and it doesn't mean I have the IQ of a blade of grass. Speaking of dealing with haters, turn the page to learn one of my favorite responses when someone serves me a cold glass of haterade with some waaa-mburgers and French cries.

Deal with it.

"WAHHH-WAHHH! ADHD SOUNDS LIKE A COP-OUT! TOUGH IS WRITING A PAPER ON MONGOLIAN TRIBAL STRUCTURE UNDER ENEMY FIRE!"

Six Words That Go Great Together

One of my favorite phrases is

"You$_{(1)}$ do$_{(2)}$ you,$_{(3)}$ I'll$_{(4)}$ do$_{(5)}$ me."$_{(6)}$

Now, "You do you, I'll do me" is a pretty powerful phrase. You throw it at your boyfriend, girlfriend, parent, or boss, and you could get slapped or fired. What "You do you, I'll do me" is meant for is when someone wants you to explain or defend something—especially something personal—that really doesn't concern him or her. Do I need to justify the color of my shoelaces? If after talking with my doctor and family, do I really need to defend to some random stranger why I'm taking a certain medication? Does the gas station attendant really need to know why I like eating honey out of a jar? People love to question anything different and insert their opinion into things that don't really affect them.

Side Note: You can also dress up "You do you, I'll do me" really nicely to avoid sounding rude. Try telling a friend of your grandparents, "I'm sorry, but I'd prefer not to discuss this issue with you." That's like "You do you, I'll do me" in a collared shirt and bow tie. You can also add a little humor to soften the blow.

Since "You do you, I'll do me" is so powerful, people wonder if there is any way to defeat it. Can scissors beat rock? Can rock beat paper? What if you have a good friend who does something lame like smoke cigarettes and tells you, "You do you, and I'll do me"? Well, that's easy. "You do you, I'll do me" doesn't work when:

a) that person's actions have a direct effect on you

b) the negative effect of the action or decision in question is beyond repute

So telling your friend to stop smoking cigarettes is more powerful than "You do you, I'll do me," because your friend's secondhand smoke will have an effect on your lungs—and dirt-sticks are disgusting (beyond repute).

Anyway, you can bet your sweet britches that if you see me on the street and ask me "Jonathan, why are you wearing a professional wrestling championship belt?" you'll hear:

"You do you, I'll do me."

It Wasn't Me, It Was A-D-D!

Let's say you've had an upset stomach for a few weeks and you don't know what's going on. Then let's say you go to the doctor and the doctor says, "We found out what's up with your stomach: you ate a tainted chicken nugget. I'm going to prescribe this syrup and you should be all good." You'd be stoked to get back to normal, right?

When I found out I had ADHD, I took the diagnosis a little differently. I looked at it like the most epic excuse ever. If I knew a symptom of ADHD was having a tough time finishing assignments, then I thought it was okay to leave things incomplete: *Sorry, guys! It's my ADHD!* If I talked out of turn: *Relax, bro, according to the experts I'm SUPPOSED to blurt stuff out.*

Basically, ADHD became the ultimate hall pass for doing whatever I wanted:

o Didn't flush the toilet? . . . ADHD

o Didn't finish homework? . . . ADHD

o Didn't eat my vegetables? . . . ADHD

o Threw a water balloon at a Ferrari? . . . ADHD

At first my parents didn't know how to respond. After all, most of my excuses lined up with the symptoms in medical books. But after a week or two they kind of got over it and stopped letting things slide. Their logic was probably something like, "If the police won't accept it as an excuse, neither should we." ADHD or not, homework was still due, chores were still required, and the dog still needed to be walked. I couldn't get away with saying "It's ADHD" to get out of stuff.

The good thing about getting diagnosed was learning why I struggled so much with homework and paying attention in school. I also learned things I could do to make that stuff easier. Like the old G.I. Joe cartoons said, "Now you know, and knowing is half the battle!"

I would drive slower if I *could*, but I have this special brain, see, and . . .

Tell it to the judge, buddy.

KEEPING IT REAL

I've never been an officially certified gangsta', and I didn't really grow up in the 'hood, but I'm pretty sure I used to keep it real with the best of them. I kept it really real; in fact, I kept it so real that I would automatically speak whatever was on my mind. If I thought dinner was bad, I'd mention it, or if I thought your dress was cool, I'd tell you. And if you wondered why that person wouldn't go out with you, I'd tell you what everyone else was afraid to say. I was like a car with a straight pipe from the motor to the exhaust—no muffler. If the gears were spinning, you'd hear them.

Keeping it so real was a double-edged sword. When I said something nice, people appreciated it because it was genuine. But when I said something not-so-nice, people got bummed because they knew I wasn't holding back. I liked having people appreciate my compliments, but I felt really bad when I unintentionally bummed someone out.

Refined Weapon: I know a lot of special brains suffer from Automatically Keeping It Real (AKIR) syndrome. I used to suffer from AKIR syndrome, but I decided to turn into a "semi-automatically keeping it real" person. Semi-autos are a lot safer than autos and aren't as dangerous to bring to job interviews or first dates.

I've learned to speak from the heart when it's something positive or if someone explicitly asks for my opinion. I try to evaluate every statement before it leaves my mouth, like a muffler from the engine to the exhaust. If we're talking about something that is too late to change (like a badly cooked meal or a poor athletic performance) or something that's really personal (like having a stupid tattoo), then I figure keeping it real won't do anything but hurt feelings (which sucks).

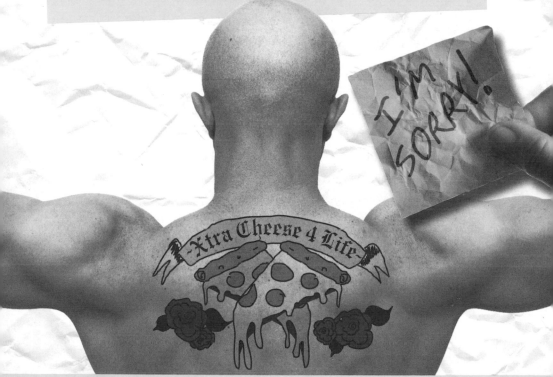

Sometimes my brain likes to talk a lot. I know you're not supposed to engage in conversation in the library, at the movies, or during wedding vows, but sometimes I just like to ask people how they're doing.

Even though I like to chitchat, when I study I need it to be super quiet. I can get distracted really easily, so if two bugs are making a racket or the trees are whistling too much in the wind, it can wreck my train of thought. I know that sounds like a double standard: "You never shut up when *you* want to talk, but when you want quiet, you won't let anyone else talk!" Yeah, that's true. That brings up another good point . . .

. . . I bet it would be cool if I looked like Mr. T, because when Mr. T says something, everyone listens. So when Mr. T wants quiet, everyone gets quiet, and when Mr. T wants to talk, everyone talks. I should probably hit the gym and bulk up on protein shakes.

Advice: If you can get the gold chains, Mohawk, and massive build to look like Mr. T, then it shouldn't be much of an issue intimidating fools into talking or being quiet (whatever your preference). But the rest of us have to look at other solutions. For most people this is probably basic, but for special brains, we have to first consider whether a specific place is acceptable for striking up conversations. Religious services, libraries, and movie theaters aren't good places to talk to random people, because most likely 99 percent of the people around you aren't there to small talk. A good way to figure it out would be to ask yourself, "If I started singing Guns N' Roses right now, would the majority of the people be kind of cool with it . . . or angry?" If they'd be angry, it might not be the best place to chitchat.

When it comes to finding a place that's quiet where it's easy to focus, I always feel the more secluded, the better. It's like I'm playing a game of hide-and-seek with distraction. If I can find a place where distraction won't find me, I win. So if you find a tiny crevice near the back patio that gets a visitor once every three years, that's probably an insane little study spot. Also, if you get really distracted by the Internet (and you don't need it for whatever assignment you're working on), see if being disconnected helps your productivity.

In this corner, weighing in at 1,000 pounds, the gorilla in the room, the dominating distraction, the titan of time wasting, Mr. Wasted-three-hours-looking-at-rain-boots . . .

. . . the Internet!

THE 7:30 TO 3:30

School is a really difficult place for people with ADHD. A high percentage of special brains get in trouble or suspended, some of us even expelled. It's pretty easy to see why. Nobody I know gets on the school bus thinking, "Man, I really want to get the worst grade possible on my quiz today." But sitting in a desk, learning about things that may not be interesting, and not being allowed to goof around are constricting for any kid—especially for someone with ADHD.

Some things in school I struggled with no matter how hard I tried. Some lectures were so painful I wanted to rip my skin off and throw it at the window. I'm not watering that down either! Sometimes it was because the subject would not make sense to my brain. I had some really nice math teachers, but it felt like my brain had a brick wall that stopped anything they tried to teach me. Other times it was a teacher who couldn't handle that I would get a little more excited and talkative than the other students. These teachers misread my talking out of turn as being disruptive instead of being enthusiastic.

When I was in middle school, I had an arts and crafts teacher who gave me a C+ because she felt I didn't follow directions well and I would frequently move around the class and check out what other people were making. In reality, I liked to be really creative and experiment with things, and I was very inquisitive about seeing what other people were up to.

After getting a C+, I assumed that all the things she said about me had to be true (she's a teacher, right?), and when it came to art I was C+ material. It took me about eight more years to finally get an art set and decide to paint something. While the stuff I drew wasn't going into a museum, I discovered how much I really love painting. I let that teacher's bad grade take away eight years that I could have been making stuff. WEAK! Some teachers have a tough time dealing with special brains and write them off completely. If you have an art teacher whose name rhymes perfectly with the word "satan" (like mine did—true story), don't let grades dictate whether you can or can't be an artist.

On a more general level, just because you may struggle with school doesn't mean life will always be like that. Don't worry, very few jobs are landed based on your ability to divide polynomials.

The Class—icks

The Declaration of Independence doesn't apply to school subjects, because all subjects are *not* created equal! Unfortunately, you'll probably have to take a class that is as pleasant to you as a goat in a sauna (since a goat in a sauna probably isn't that pleasant).

So relA-A-A-A-A-xing!

Most school districts and colleges have pretty straightforward requirements. You probably are expected to achieve competency in English, science, math, and a foreign language. These requirements often are a lot more open to interpretation than you may think, so it's a good idea to work with a guidance counselor or an administrator to see what options are available to meet them.

For example, I fulfilled a large chunk of my science requirements taking classes on astronomy and natural disasters. Learning about earthquakes and black holes was pretty mellow. My brother found out he could take sign language (or ASL) for his foreign language requirements. It was a smart move because my brother can communicate with a lot of cool deaf people, and now he's got a skill that not many people have. Plus he can say inappropriate things without people hearing!

COMIC BOOK CLASS

EVERY CLASS I TOOK IN COLLEGE FOLLOWED THE SAME FORMULA: BIG ASSIGNMENT, MIDTERM, BIG ASSIGNMENT, FINAL EXAM (OR AT LEAST SOME VARIATION OF THE FORMULA).

MY SENIOR YEAR I ENROLLED IN A COMIC BOOK ANALYSIS CLASS FOR AN ENGLISH ELECTIVE REQUIREMENT. HAVING HAD JUST ABOUT ENOUGH OF WRITING PAPERS, ON A WHIM I ASKED THE PROFESSOR (WHO WAS THIS REALLY NICE GUY WITH A TON OF TATTOOS HEAD TO TOE) IF I COULD EXPRESS MY OPINIONS WITH MY PAINTINGS INSTEAD OF PAPERS. HE SAID YES, AND FOR THE FIRST TIME IN MY COLLEGE CAREER I GOT AN A IN A CLASS (I EVEN GOT A C+ IN YOGA).

IDEA!

I CAN ONLY IMAGINE IF I HAD ADOPTED THIS STRATEGY IN KINDERGARTEN INSTEAD OF SENIOR YEAR IN COLLEGE — CAN YOU SAY "DEAN'S LIST"?

IN ALL SERIOUSNESS, I HAD SO MANY ASSIGNMENTS WHERE I COULD HAVE EXPRESSED MYSELF BETTER IN A PAINTING OR VIDEO THAN AN ESSAY. YOU'LL PROBABLY GET SHOT DOWN 9 TIMES OUT OF 10, BUT IF YOU CAN DO ONE DIORAMA/ORAL REPORT/INTERPRETIVE DANCE/ETC. INSTEAD OF DOING SOMETHING YOU'RE NOT GOOD AT, THEN IT'S WORTH CHECKING INTO.

I DON'T THINK YOU CAN CONVINCE THE COLLEGE BOARD (WHO CREATES THE SAT) TO LET YOU DO A PUPPET SHOW INSTEAD OF THE WRITING PORTION OF THE TEST, BUT I'D LOVE FOR SOMEONE TO PROVE ME WRONG. ANYWAY, THE MORAL OF THE STORY IS: IT NEVER HURTS TO ASK!

Yeah, That's Going to Be a Problem

Starting homework was always really difficult. After the final bell rang, my brain was toast (and it's never a good idea to re-toast toast). I spent countless evenings staring at homework problems trying to pep talk my brain into getting started.

Homework is something anybody with a high school degree had to do. Even after high school, you'll encounter things you won't be hyped on, like jury duty, flu shots, or picking up after your dog. I can't help with your jury duty or dog poop, but here are some tips for homework.

Tips: Homework is supposed to be like the gym for your brain. It's not efficient to go to the gym for four hours and do only five jumping jacks.

- If one subject is taking you all night (when it should only take a half hour), then that's an issue. Approach the teacher about creating (or altering) assignments, so you aren't spending too long on stuff. Talk to the teacher when nobody else is around, so he or she won't feel pressure to hold the line in front of other students.

- Check your environment. A 40-minute homework assignment can turn into three hours if you switch between the TV, phone, and stray magazines. It's way easier to go hard for one hour and finish your homework than it is to put in a compromised effort and spend a few hours on it.

- Ask for help. Find out if your school has tutoring or homework services. Check your local library, Boys and Girls Clubs, YMCA, even church, synagogue, or mosque, to see if they offer any type of homework assistance. Having someone next to you keeping you on task is a huge help.

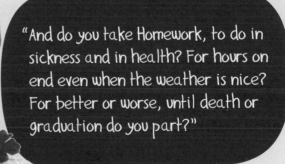

"And do you take Homework, to do in sickness and in health? For hours on end even when the weather is nice? For better or worse, until death or graduation do you part?"

TAKING A TEST AT THE SPEED OF A TUMBLEWEED

If you have ADHD, you are probably eligible for extended time to take tests. Most school districts and standardized tests (like the SAT) have rules that say you qualify for it. When I did this, a lot of people thought ADHD was something I made up to get special treatment. It wasn't. Even if I'm taking a really important test and I'm really focused, I still have a bunch of random ideas that pop in and out of my head. It's not very fun when you are fingers deep in a math final and start thinking about medieval jousting. After thinking about how you would look in metal armor for a few moments, suddenly you realize . . . OH SNAP! I need to get back into these math problems.

Of course, having to continually refocus and trying to be as accurate as possible for that long can really take a toll. After whipping my brain into focus on an extended-time test, it seriously feels like I've done a workout (which is sort of lame, 'cause brains don't get six-pack abs).

I strongly suggest arranging extended time on finals and important tests. I figure it's better to have it and not need it than to need it and not have it. Sort of like a vaccine for the chicken pox. But setting everything up and getting your teachers on board with your extended-time program typically doesn't happen overnight. Talk with an academic advisor and your doctor early in the school year (or as soon as you qualify) to get everything cleared for extended time. I know the College Board requires you to have a bunch of documents for the SAT, so get on it. (Go to www.collegeboard.com or google "SAT accommodations" for more info.) It's pretty lame that they ask for so much stuff, but I don't make the rules.

Side Note: One thing that is sort of a drag about extended time is having to take the test by yourself in the library or in a special place for extended-time students. It can feel pretty ostracizing and uncomfortable. Still, testing in a special place can be a great way to avoid distractions (see page 20), and I really needed the extended time for a few of my exams. You probably will, too.

> I seek the realm of extended time. Dost thou knoweth the way?

Square Peg, Round Hole

Having a special brain isn't like having a normal suit-and-tie brain. We're the same species, but different breeds. It's like having a Great Dane and a Chihuahua. You may have all these ideas about how to raise a Great Dane, but if you get a Chihuahua, you're going to have to adjust your strategies a bit. There are so many people out there trying to raise Chihuahuas like Great Danes.

It's not like special brains need constant help to learn most things. Nobody had to coddle me to learn how to ride a bike or become potty trained. I'd say 75 percent of the things I've learned in my life didn't require me to be treated any different from a suit-and-tie brain. The remaining 25 percent just required different strategies.

Maybe I needed something explained twice (or five or six times), or maybe someone showed me a different way to solve a problem. It wasn't the end of the world. All I had to do was ask, and the overwhelming majority of the time it has helped me learn difficult stuff.

⭐ Do This: If you don't understand something, ask to have it explained again or shown to you in a different way. Most teachers are familiar with ADHD and have a pretty good idea of how to reach us. Most other adults, like coaches and parents, know what it is as well, and they're happy to help. If you deal with someone who belittles you for needing extra help, just tell them you had a rough night or don't feel well. There's no use arguing with ill-informed adults who don't understand why some people may learn differently from the majority.

Tell Me What You Want
(Whatcha Really, Really Want)

I hate when someone gives me a task that's not very clear. If you tell me to clean my room, that's pretty vague. Do you mean pick up the dirty clothes? Does that include emptying my trash can? Am I supposed to vacuum the floor? Do you want me to move everything out, clean it with Windex, and then put everything back? Should I get crazy with cotton swabs and turn my room into a sterile chamber?

I don't do well with chores that are open to multiple interpretations. Either I assume way too much, and go above and beyond what is expected (bumming me out), or I assume way too little (bumming out whoever assigned me the task).

Whenever someone tells me to do something and I'm unsure, I ask that person to be specific about his expectations. You want me to answer the phones at a job, tell me what you want me to say. You want me to wash your car? You want inside, outside, wax, or no wax? It's like the old saying, when you *assume* you make an ASS out of U and ME.

(get it? It spells "assume.")

Subjects of Death

I can't prove that nobody has died from Algebra 2 or Biology. I know I used to look over my homework and yell, "This stuff is going to kill me!" Even though it didn't kill *me*, it is possible some poor kid somewhere sometime did die from Algebra 2 or Bio homework.

When I say Bio or Algebra 2, think of those classes that almost killed you. I am referring to any class that was ridiculously difficult and unnatural for you, like Bio and Algebra 2 were for me. Even if I tried my very hardest in those classes, I would be stoked if I got a C. I kept thinking, "Why should I care?" It was like getting sucker punched when I would see other kids in the class barely study and get grades that were equal to or better than mine.

"Hey, Sally, I spent the last three nights making flash cards and all this other stuff for this exam, and I got a 71 percent. I'm so glad I didn't go skateboarding with my friends or watch TV so that I could really do my best."

"Oh, hey, Jonathan, I actually forgot about the test today. I was too busy skateboarding, watching TV, and hanging out with all the cool people. I'm so bummed I got an 84."

The goal of this book is to show special brains how it's actually kind of rad being born with a special brain. Unfortunately, for all the great things that come with our membership, also come a few bummers. Some of those bummers will be classes that require maximum effort with minimum reward.

On the flipside of the coin, most of us have plenty to be thankful for. It really is crushing to spend all this time and effort learning things that your brain seems allergic to, but it's just part of life. It's horrible failing a class after trying hard all year (I know from experience), but life moves on. Special brains (like anyone) need to learn that life has its ups and downs. Sometimes it seems like the bad days never end . . . but eventually they always do (and that's when it's time to go outside and celebrate!).

R.I.P.
RANDOM STUDENT
1996–2012
TOO MUCH MATH

poulet

chicken

Side Note: Failing a certain subject (or subjects) is not the same as being a failure. Special brains are not meant to be Swiss Army knives (decent at everything)—we are surgeons' scalpels! We were meant to do great things, things that don't involve the subjects we hate. If we get teased because we had to study 10 hours to barely pass a class . . . whatever, we passed. (That's what's important.) You think guys like Rambo worry about being teased for barely passing French class? They don't! So what if Rambo had to make tons of flash cards or use a bunch of highlighters just to get a C-. Now Rambo is too busy doing special-brain-type stuff like playing in the forest and shooting arrows at the haters.

K.
I'm outta here.

A POSITIVE PERSPECTIVE ON SCHOOL

I don't know who created the modern concept of school. Back in the day, kids went to school for only a few years. If you made it past the sixth grade, you were a pretty big deal (Abe Lincoln was rumored to have only a year and a half of formal education). Times have changed. That's probably good, because 200 years ago life was a lot harder.

Since we no longer need to defend our stagecoach from attacking mountain lions, we might as well learn to accept that most of us will be in school until we are at least 17 or 18 years old. Like anything, high school is what you make of it.

You can look at high school as a place to:

- Meet kids from the neighborhood, learn how to make out, and make friendships that last a long time

- Learn about things that interest you (and find out what you're interested in)

- Perfect your acting skills when it comes to faking sick on exam days

"You have ~~dysentery~~ homework."

TV

I always get bummed when people say TV is bad for you. TV isn't bad for you; rat poison and undercooked chicken are bad for you.

TV is a lot like a burrito. If you haven't discovered this amazing creation, a burrito is like a meal with a tortilla wrapped around it. If you fill your burrito with fresh, healthy ingredients, it's good for you. But if you eat those nasty premade microwave burritos that are filled with processed junk, that's bad for you. If you eat enough of them, you'll probably weigh 300 pounds and put your health in serious jeopardy.

The same goes for TV. Depending on what you watch, TV can be a really healthy or really unhealthy part of your diet. If you watch well-made, informative shows, you can learn a lot. But if you sit around and watch stupid stuff on TV all day, you'll turn your brain and your body into mush.

A good way to determine if you are watching garbage is to do what I call "The Grandma Test." Imagine telling your grandma (if you don't have one, imagine a stereotypical grandmother) about the show you are watching. Her reaction can tell you if the show is good for you . . . or not.

Brain Pep Talk

Nobody likes getting a bad grade on a test or getting rejected by someone they like. When I get a bad result, my first reaction is to take it *really* personally. For me, it's not just a bad grade on a math exam; it's a statement about who I am as a person. It feels like I've built this nice sand castle out of all my achievements, and the math exam was a giant rock that smashed the castle to pieces!

Over the years, I've worked really hard to make my castle more smash-proof (adding a moat and some cement to the mix). Whenever I get bummed, I just remember something good that happened or something nice someone said to me. When someone I don't care about criticizes me, I don't let it sink in very deep. If I have a bad day of fishing, I take it as an isolated incident so it doesn't have to turn into a bad week of fishing. And when I get negative feedback on something I did, I try not to let it make me doubt the good feedback I've received.

It's a fine line to avoid being cocky, but it doesn't hurt to remind your brain of all its past achievements. Back in the day, getting rejected by someone used to ruin all the memories of anyone who did like me. Now when some girl decides she doesn't want to get smoothies with me, I remind myself of all the girls I did take out for smoothies.

FREAKING OUT

Whenever I want to do something ambitious (like try to become an astronaut, sell something I made in a store, or open a meat pie shop), people try to encourage me by saying, "Go for it, what's the worst that could happen?" Well, sometimes the answer in my mind is, "A lot!"

Say I want to paint a portrait of a goldfish and sell it. In reality, probably the worst that can happen is I spend some money on paint and a canvas, get told no by a few gallery owners, and try again. But in my mind the worst that can happen is being homeless, laughed out of town, and humiliated online as a result of creating a janky goldfish painting.

A lot of people may think, "That's ridiculous, you're overreacting," and that's true. But if I let my thoughts go unchecked, I can get so freaked out over venturing into uncharted territory that all I can think about is the horrible things that "may" happen (getting eaten by piranhas, put on CNN with the words "failure" above me, etc.).

Sometimes I get so paralyzed with the fear of failure, I forget to think about the chance of good things happening if I try. Lately, my goal has been to keep reality closer in mind before I start freaking out. So before I start thinking about how ordering fish tacos might make me too full to eat Chinese food at my favorite place later . . . I take a deep breath and tell myself, "Jonathan, relax. You're just having lunch. You can worry about dinner later." Odds are the world will keep on spinning.

click to find out!

FIRST ATTEMPT DEEMED "UTTER FAILURE" BY CRITICS AND CONFECTIONISTS ALIKE

👍 6,456,151 People Like This

Guests attending the annual _Neighborhood Arts Jam_ at _Mamacita's Coffee & Bakery_ left with a bad taste in their mouth after the cafe/gallery debuted a painting titled _Left Finned_, a rudimentary depiction of a pet goldfish constructed out of canvas, acrylic paint, and permanent marker.

The piece, displayed in an ornate gold frame, was priced to sell at $125, or best offer. Descriptions of the painting by attendees ranged from "unfortunate" to "dishcartening." One patron even referred to it as "an obvious practical joke." In fact, _Left Finned_ was so unpopular that, although seating was limited, a couch underneath the wall space that the painting occupied remained vacant the entire evening.

COMMENT

LOLWUT?

my dog can paint better! LOL

Is you dog's name Fido by chance? :) :) :)

I spent $300,000 for a fine arts educatoin and, yeah, stuff like really this ticks me off.

this^

You should ask for a refund cuz you obviously never learned to spell.

^^^^troll^^^^   show 46 replies

I hear he made bad meat pies 2

I MEAN......YOU CAN BUY A REAL GOLDFISH FOR LIKE $1!!!!!!!!!

WHO WOULD BUY A PAINTING OF A FREAKIN' GOLDFISH!!!!!!

quiet please.

x cuts..._Breaking: Jonathan Chesner not very good at painting goldfish_...Wall Str

JOBS

When I was writing this book and explained to people that I was making the best book ever on ADHD, they always responded with, "Oh, I have a sister/cousin/roommate/girlfriend/boyfriend/brother with that."

When I asked what their brother/mother/cousin/roommate/girlfriend/boyfriend/mailman does, a few of the answers were pretty amazing. Judging from the responses I got, I don't think there is an occupation that doesn't have a few special-brained people doing it. I've met special brains who are foreign language experts, investment bankers, scientists, doctors, and firefighters.

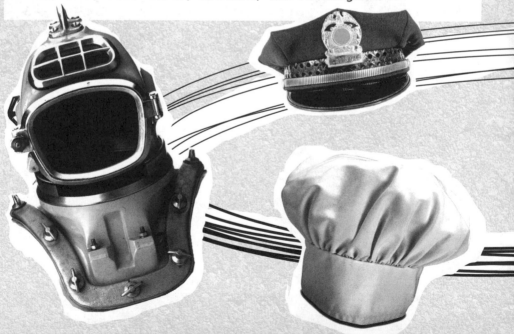

One of the cool things about having a special brain is that you can get really caught up in things. A lot of special brains become really successful because they become almost obsessed with learning or achieving something. Think about something that really excites or interests you. If you're like me, it's not very difficult to invest tons of time learning or doing it. Are you really interested in being a doctor? Med school, schmed school—piece of cake!

Why Rules Exist

I learned to speak in fluid sentences before I was two years old, so before you read this and call me stupid, don't forget that.

Anyway, I learned that rules served a purpose when I was roughly 22 years old. It wasn't because I got arrested or anything, it just sort of dawned on me one day that if everybody did what they wanted to do, things might get a little dangerous. I don't want people with monster trucks cutting in line at the drive-thru or my neighbors raising crocodiles in their pool.

Hold the Fern

Most awesome things, like a lightsaber, can be a weapon for good (like when Yoda or Luke Skywalker used them) or for bad (like if my little brother had one). While I'm sure most of us would be very responsible with our lightsabers (and never use them to open soup cans or carve our initials into trees), it'd be tough to resist the temptation to mess around with them occasionally.

I don't have a lightsaber, but I do have lots of excellent things that can be detrimental to my productivity. Here's a list:

- Cell phone

- Rap music

- Fishing rod

- Pet fern

Whenever I have serious work to do, I move everything that can become a distraction to a different room or turn it off. I know it used to bum out my fern bush✻, but even it needed to hang out somewhere else. I even told the plant, "If I can't focus, the bills ain't getting paid, and you're getting planted in the alley."

You'll be amazed at how much easier it is to focus when you do this. You can get all your work done in half the time it would take if you were distracted, and that leaves you hours on end to respond to text messages from pop stars and to spend quality time with your fern.

DREAMLAND

I have the most racy imagination ever. Not racy as in thinking of girls in underwear all day, but racy as in it likes to race. Here's a typical situation:

I'm sitting at my desk doing homework and look over at my watch. My watch is a pretty rad dive watch and I like how it says "Made in Japan." I want to go to Japan. I really like sushi, too. How good is that one sushi restaurant near that movie theater? I'm excited to see that new movie with the guy who played Indiana Jones's dad. Oh, remember when I was working in LA and saw the guy who tried to steal the gold statue from Indy in *Raiders of the Lost Ark*? That was super random, and I got to ring up Owen Wilson. How funny is that video of him skateboarding? Speaking of skateboarding, I need to fix my board since it got run over by a car. I'm going to call the local shop back home . . .

So by taking a break from doing my homework to see what time it was, I ended up on the phone with my local skate shop asking if they have any cool skateboard decks with pictures of Japanese stuff on them. An hour later, I'm racking my brain trying to remember what I needed to get done.

So my watch says Made in Japan . . . I've always wanted to go to Japan to eat.

How fun would it be to catch your own sushi?

. . . maybe later. What time is it?

Which is totally possible since I got a fishing rod for my birthday!

Oh yeah, I need to hit the grocery store for lunch fixings . . .

And I can't wait to use it on my friend's boat! Which reminds me, it was so cool when I rode in a boat to that one place!

How great was that sandwich I packed?

Jonathan's Life: Opinions are like armpits (everybody has a couple), so you shouldn't live your life according to what my armpits think. That being said, one of the reasons I choose to take medication is to help prevent my brain from drifting off. I feel like my medication gives my brain better brake pads to help It slow down when it starts to get rambunctious.

The Doc

There are lots of special brains who don't have ADHD. Among special brains who do have ADHD, there's a ton who don't take medication. But if you're a special brain, you have ADHD, and you take (or plan to take) medication, you may have to see a psychiatrist to get it.*

I know I'm not the only one who didn't like the concept of seeing a shrink. A lot of people assume that if you see a psychiatrist you must be super depressed or a little crazy. Obviously, people see psychiatrists to talk about all types of stuff, but I was worried people would think I was perma-bummed or not right in the head. I had no urge to go, and for a long time I avoided it.

Just open up and say . . .

But once it started getting too hard to focus in school, I decided to go. After a few visits, I realized the psychiatrist was not all that bad. If a friend found out that I had gone to a psychiatrist, I explained that a psychiatrist is the only one authorized to prescribe my meds. My doctor was actually a pretty cool guy (he even wrote the foreword for this book). We'd discuss how my medication was treating me, and how things were going at school and with friends, etc. He'd let me talk about whatever I wanted. If I wanted to discuss how effective my prescriptions were, we'd do that. If I wanted advice about something, he'd offer his opinion. I actually appreciate all the help he gave me while I was in school.

Psychiatrists are often underappreciated. Everyone hypes up neurosurgeons because of how much skill it requires to operate on a brain. Well, psychiatrists may not be flipping back scalps, but they work on brains, too.

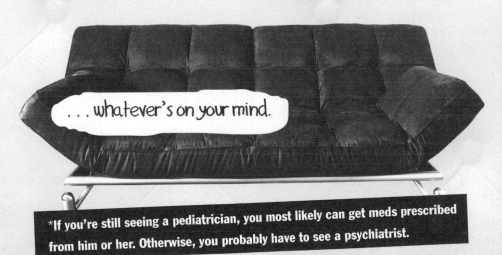

. . . whatever's on your mind.

*If you're still seeing a pediatrician, you most likely can get meds prescribed from him or her. Otherwise, you probably have to see a psychiatrist.

LOOKING AROUND

Sometimes special brains take a lot of flak because our brains want to look around so much. For whatever reason, it irritates people when our heads are on a swivel. Irritating or not, I like to see what's going on around me every time I'm sitting in an auditorium or at the movies. People are super interesting. Besides, if some guy had a heart attack during a movie, and a special brain wasn't there doing recon all over the place, he'd probably die. But if a special brain was around, he'd probably live because the special brain would notice and call 911.

Some say easily distracted, I say keenly observant. Toh-may-tow, Toh-mah-tow.

One time I was surfing in northern Los Angeles. Everyone around me was focused, waiting for waves to come, while I was looking all over the place as usual. Some girl came running into the water with all her clothes on and started to drown. Who noticed? Who saved her life? Yeah, the distracted kid! Thanks, special brain! Straight up David Hasselhoff *Baywatch* status! So maybe our special brains are meant to help save someone's life. You never know when having a special brain will come in handy!

RADNESS!

clap   clap   clap   clap

$v_f = v_2 + at$

If it's presented in a cool enough way, my brain can get stoked about almost anything. Even the most random thing, like curling. It's this obscure Olympic sport where (from what I can gather) a stone is pushed across a patch of ice and curlers try to direct its path with brooms. We didn't have much ice growing up in San Diego, but even if we did, I don't think curling would sound that exciting. But when you add announcers, multiple camera angles, on-screen statistics, and more . . . curling becomes kind of rad!

It got me thinking, what if science or history classes were presented in a more interesting way? I've always found that watching a medical drama or crime scene show makes science seem much cooler than listening to a lecture on paramecia. I never really got down with physics, but when I learned how important physics is to improving my cannonball technique, it made it seem a lot more relevant and interesting.

Class: Buckle Up, It Might Get Bumpy

In my high school days, I wanted to sit in the back of the class with all the cool kids. I remember watching *The Fresh Prince of Bel-Air* when I was younger, and Will Smith always used to sit in the back (and if Will Smith jumped off a bridge, obviously at 15 I would have, too). I sat in the back a few times trying to be like Will Smith, but it was too hard for my brain to focus on the teacher. There was so much stuff for my brain to notice from the back of the classroom! I could check out the posters, other kids' sneakers, the teacher's desk. Oh, and don't get me started on staring out the classroom windows. My brain loves staring out the window and watching people cross the street. It's the same thing with watching ants (they're always doing stuff, it's really entertaining).

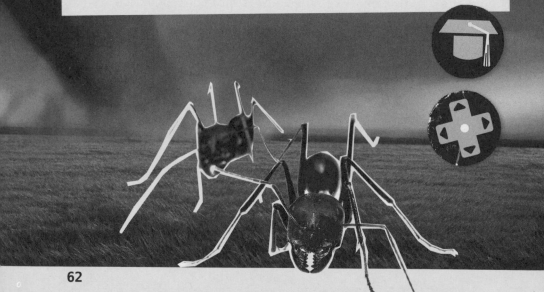

Brilliant! I came to the conclusion that I have to sit somewhere close to the front. Even if my brain only focuses on the teacher for half the class, that's better than it did when I sat in the back. A few slices of cake are better than none (I like chocolate cake with vanilla frosting). Think about your peripheral vision from the back of the class—pretty easy to get distracted? Moving to the front cuts your peripheral vision way down (meaning less things to sidetrack you).

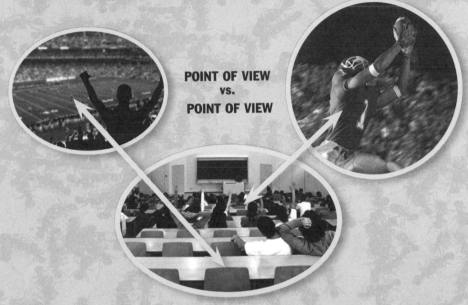

POINT OF VIEW
vs.
POINT OF VIEW

Side Note: All those things that distract you in your peripheral vision are called "tornados." Tornados suck you into what they're doing and distract you for the whole class period. Tornados can be other kids goofing off in class or even just a student walking past the window outside. Sit next to tornados if you want to know whatever is *not* going to be on the test and/or you want to get in trouble. (So basically don't sit next to them.)

Right When I Start Getting Good

Oh my gosh, this fully bums me out to no end: I'll be in class and my brain is learning how to solve problems a certain way. Finally, about 30 minutes into it, my brain feels like it's just starting to understand what's going on. Like if I had 10 minutes more, I'd be a pro at whatever it is we're learning. Then the teacher decides to throw something new onto the board—totally change the subject—and my brain is like, "Whaaaa? Hold up! I didn't even master the previous thing! . . . uhhh . . . YOU TRIPPIN'." (Seriously, that's pretty much verbatim what my brain thinks.)

Having a special brain often means that certain things will take longer to learn. Being five minutes behind in whatever you're learning is a pain in the butt when the teacher moves on to something new. It's like everyone is following each other downtown in cars and I'm five minutes behind. It's all fun and games when we're on a straightaway, but once the teacher throws a hard right turn, my brain gets lost.

I guess it's only fair that some things take forever to learn, because other things come really quick for special brains. While it might have taken me a long time to understand verb conjugations, I was an absolute beast when it came to learning to use the DVD player remote at my parents' house. So even though some things can take forever to learn, I'm still the only one in my family who knows how to turn on a DVD without getting up.

How do you do that??

Magic.

FADE TO CHINESE

I love Chinese people and their food, so this isn't anything against Chinese people.

On an average school day, around 11:30 (right before lunch) and again around 2:00 (right before school was done) I'd find that my teachers were speaking Chinese*. They'd be going on and on about *Macbeth* or something, and I kid you not, they might as well have been speaking Chinese. And you know what sucks even more? Whatever they were speaking about was probably going to be on a test eventually, but since it sounded like Chinese, I wasn't getting any of it.

13. 为什么要暗杀国王邓肯?

    a. 他吃了我的三明治

    b. 三女巫的预言

    c. 降低税收

    d. 失去了赌注

    e. 所有上述

14. 是什么时候

    a. 没有足够的信

    b. 在哪一年?

    c. 它取决于季节

    d. 除以三

*If you are special brained and speak Chinese, then substitute Swahili for Chinese in my example. And if you are special brained and speak both Chinese and Swahili, then substitute hieroglyphics (yes, I know they are written and not spoken).

Good Ideas:

There is no single cause for feeling like your teacher is speaking Chinese, and you can't turn on your focus like a switch. That being said, here are some things you can do during the school day that may help.

- **Check your diet.** Getting a cheeseburger and soda isn't the best way to pregame for an afternoon of learning. Soda has tons of sugar and artificial ingredients and a cheeseburger isn't exactly the meal of champions. A healthy lunch will provide lots more energy so you can focus better. Also sneak a low-sugar cereal bar or some fruit midmorning to carry you through to lunch.

- **Look into medication.** This is exactly the kind of thing it's good for. (See page 56.)

- **Get physical.** Walk around or find a good hiding spot to do push-ups and jumping jacks during break to avoid getting restless later. Research says that exercise even helps your brain grow stronger and be better able to focus.

- **Borrow notes.** Ask if you can look at a friend's notes to fill in the gaps while you tuned out.

- **Alert a friend.** Ask a friend to tap you out of dreamland whenever he notices you zoning out.

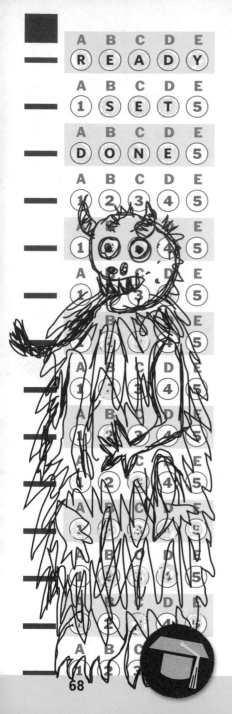

	A	B	C	D	E
	R	E	A	D	Y

	A	B	C	D	E
	1	S	E	T	5

	A	B	C	D	E
	D	O	N	E	5

I don't think the world understands what it's like having ADHD and trying to take a test or quiz. A quiz might not hold our attention as well as watching two bears fighting over a trout. Once you muster up all your focus to get through a question, you don't ever want to see that question again. It's like speed dating in a room full of grumpy people—hurry up and move on. That's why it's so hard to double-check answers: I just put all this effort into getting through those questions, and you want me to reintroduce myself to them again?

A	B	C	D	E		A	B	C	D	E
A	D	V	I	C	E	E	2	3	4	5

ADHD brains can be pretty decisive sometimes. We either like something (like ninja hamsters) or we don't (like polka music). Bam! Decision made. But always try to double-check your work! I've caught some really stupid errors of mine by double-checking.

A B C D E   A B C D E   A B C D E
(M)(O)(R)(E)(5) (A)(D)(V)(I)(C)(E)(2)(3)(4)(5)

If you already double-checked (or if double-checking will make you dry heave), then *do not* start drawing or scribbling on the test or the answer sheet! You would think a teacher would be excited to receive the test back with a giant drawing of a rabid pandadactyl (panda/ pterodactyl), but it only makes the teacher grade you more stringently. To the teacher, if you had enough time to draw a rabid pandadactyl, then you should have had enough time to get all the questions right. I suggest using a piece of scratch paper to draw animal portraits, play word games, and practice your signature. That way you can throw away the scratch paper and not bum out your teacher with a test filled with random monsters and creatures.

A B C D E   A B C D E   A B C D E
(A)(D)(V)(I)(C)(E)(2)(3)(4)(5)(1)(2)(3)(4)(5)

As awesome as pandadactyls, liongators, and all other hybrid creatures are, nothing can replace a good old double-check, especially for special brains. The best way to think about it is, "Hey, I really don't have anything better to do than double-check my answers right now." Sometimes you have to tell your brain that it won't die if it has to go over some questions one more time. Unless turning in the test early is the only way you'll make your flight to Hawaii, try to take your time.

Foot Tapping for Health and Wellness

Why do so many ADHD brains fidget? I don't know. Did Adam and Eve ever hang out with dinosaurs? Does it matter? Could Adam have checked out other places besides Eden if he'd ridden on the back of a pterodactyl?

I have a feeling special brains have been tapping their feet since we were huddled in caves having a meeting about how to take down a woolly mammoth. Personally, I'm a foot-tapper. It gives me something to do, feels soothing, and gives my right ankle and calf a fuller and more defined muscle structure.

Like most things I find awesome (country music, yo mama jokes, and being barefoot), not everyone agrees. Sometimes we can become oblivious to how fast and noisy our RFT (rapid foot tapping) gets. At school, students and teachers can become so awestruck with how fast we tap our foot that we become "a distraction" and are told to stop. I don't advocate tapping your foot at such a rapid pace that you get in trouble. You might have to learn to be more subtle (see "The Stealth Tap"). And if you are going to tap your foot, be productive about it. Build muscle, improve coordination, or get creative.

RFT is a common (but not exclusive) manifestation of an ADHD brain's need to stay active. If you don't tap your foot it's no big deal. If you tap your pencil, substitute RPT (rapid pencil tapping) for RFT (rapid foot tapping).

Foot tapping is a very open style. If you bob your knees, rock heel-to-toe, or do the Charleston, it doesn't matter. Everyone can bring a unique flavor to the mix. Check out these mini-exercises:

○ **SIMON:** Simon is a memory game that is highly adaptable to feet and pencils. Start off with a pattern and see how detailed you can make it while still being able to repeat it. Example: *one tap-two taps-one tap-one tap-two taps.* Repeat.

○ **THE 80s JUKEBOX:** It's really fun to tap out the beat of your favorite 1980s song (I suggest the "Top Gun Anthem"). Think about this— maybe you can create the next really addicting song while you're sitting in geography class.

○ **RHYTHMIC TWIRLING:** Try different pencil twirls. Beginners should stick to making your pen circle around the thumb. More advanced twirlers can try to do figure eights, alternate finger twirls, and crossovers (switching hand-to-hand with your twirling). Expert twirlers can coordinate a finger twirling routine to song (also known as interpretive twirling).

○ **THE STEALTH TAP:** If the people around you are anti-tapping, that doesn't mean you have to suffer through mental anguish at your lack of tapping options. You can circle your thumb, wiggle your toes, bob your head, and do any other movement that is silent not violent.

Making Friends in the Office

Some days in high school I just couldn't connect with any of my peers. It seemed like a lot of them were pretty fair-weathered or just not into the same stuff as me. It was pretty rough getting through the day without anyone to talk to.

Since I like talking to people, I found various adults around school who were willing to rap out with me. One was the school nurse. I'm a pretty healthy kid and never really got sick, but whenever I felt that class was too much, I'd tell the teacher I had a headache and would leisurely stroll over to the nurse and talk it out for a few minutes. Other students probably thought I was dying since I went to the nurse so much, but in reality I just wanted to hang out somewhere quiet and take a break from learning. After having a little conversation, I would roll back into class refreshed and ready to start feeding my brain again.

If I had already visited the nurse that week, I'd take the long way to the bathroom and visit the maintenance man, John. John was always really encouraging and never really cared about how popular I was with other kids or whether I choked during the tennis match. I had a couple of teachers who I could visit during lunch, too. Between my computer teacher, my English teacher, the librarian (not to mention the nurse and maintenance man), I always had someone I could talk to.

In college, I wanted to find a replacement for the nurse and maintenance man, so I befriended the academic advisors. I would leave class like I had to go to the bathroom, but since I only had to pee a few times a day, I would go hang out with the girls in the academic advising office. We'd rap out about what they were up to—gossip, TV, etc. The cool part was, they would always remind me after a few minutes of hanging out that I was probably missing something important in class. I didn't even have to wear a watch to keep track of time!

Important Stuff: I want to make it perfectly clear that this book is not responsible for you cutting class. I'm merely *suggesting* that if you take a restroom break, there is nothing wrong with taking a slight detour and saying hi to a faculty friend. Sometimes it's just nice to have friends at school who aren't other students. Most of these adults have seen a lot, and they give decent advice. Adults usually have a lot better perspective on things than students, too, and adults who work in schools care about kids. I used to talk to my friend Faye in the advising office about everything from dating advice to the fluidity of my thesis statements.

Old People

Way back in the day (before telephones and MP3 players), old people used to get respect. Since there were no cars, nobody could yell at old people for driving slowly. In fact, being an old person made you "the man." Up until fairly recently, people would die from all types of gnarly stuff: being mauled by a sheep, complications from a fever, maybe even infection from a spider bite. If you made it to old age, you had to be pretty wise and tough.

Nowadays living to 80 isn't as impressive as it once was. With medicine and science as good as they are, a lot of people make it to old age despite making a lot of stupid decisions. As a result, we aren't as stoked on old people as we used to be. Plus, the fact that they get senior citizen discounts and take forever in the grocery store has caused a lot of us to be anti—old people.

Well, I'm not afraid to say that most old people are still rad. A few are grumpy and a few are crude, but by and large, everyone needs an old-person friend. It makes sense to have an old person friend for several reasons:

o They've experienced a lot of stuff. You got dating drama? Why not ask someone who has been married for more than 40 years. You need help judging a person's character? Why not get advice from someone who didn't need social media or online networks to know if someone was a hussy or a chiseler.

o Being friends with old people will help you harden up, too. You think finals are tough? Try World War II. Failing Spanish? Try showing up at Ellis Island not knowing a word of English. Plus, walking around with a metal hip and a bunch of arthritis deserves mad respect.

o Probably the most important reason to befriend an old person is because if you were old, you'd want friends, too. It's kind of boring not being able to play sports as well as you used to or having to go to the bathroom 10 times a day. I know that when I'm old, I'd like to have young people hanging out with me to keep me company.

Girls (Or Guys)

In college it seemed like all these girls I liked went out with square, boring guys. They were never interested in my special brain and me. It was like if some lady had owned purebred poodles her whole life, she was never going to randomly decide to adopt a wiener dog. It used to bum me out, because I couldn't control having the brain I had, and I felt that I was being disqualified because of something I couldn't control.

But that was all before my new life mantra: "Tomorrow has the possibility to be awesome." So if today sucks, I can go to sleep and just be like, "Tomorrow's forecast is light winds with an opportunity of awesome increasing throughout the day." That makes me sleep all right. By focusing on how the day can be really good, I tend to ignore the really bad (which makes the day end up seeming pretty good).

Oh, and Also: It's never worth dating anyone who doesn't like you for who you are now.*

Oh, and Also Again: While it's good to live like tomorrow is going to be an awesome day, don't forget to try your hardest to make today an awesome day, too!

Lookin' good, dawg!

*Repeat that in your mirror every morning!

No, Really?

You know what stoked me out super crazy? One day my brain was feeling really depressed because I read these statistics about how special brains tend to get in trouble or have a tough time doing great things in life. So I went on the Internet and searched for people with ADHD. Oh, maaaan! So many heavy hitters have special brains. Thomas Edison invented tons of stuff but was called stupid all the time! Special brains can do really crazy stuff and some of the most famous people would probably have been diagnosed with ADHD. There is no reason to get bummed or think that anything is out of reach.

Here are a few cool people with ADHD (or are believed to have had it):

Richard Branson: Founder of Virgin Airlines/Records/Galactic. British philanthropist and all-around awesome adventurer.

Agatha Christie: Best-selling novelist of all time.

Albert Einstein: $E = MC^2$. Really smart guy who failed math and had an awesome haircut.

Heartthrob to millions of girls all over the world. Good dancer, singer, and actor.

Liv Tyler: Actress who starred in the Lord of the Rings movies.

Mt. Special Brain

Also: The founders of Kinko's, now known as FedEx Office (Paul Orfalea), JetBlue Airways (David Neeleman), and Wendy's (Dave Thomas).

Girls (or Guys) Part 2

If you're still in high school, pay attention: Growing up, there were tons of really nice girls I didn't give the time of day to, because I might have thought they were dorky or awkward-looking.

But some of the raddest girls I know now were under the radar in high school, and some of raddest girls in high school have become full-on bores. Obviously, not everyone goes from a caterpillar to a butterfly, but the moral of the story is: YOU NEVER KNOW WHO WILL BECOME WHAT! Today's science nerd could be tomorrow's supermodel/nuclear physicist, which would be a ridiculous combination!

Also, there's a lot more to life than having a really hot girlfriend or boyfriend. Don't get me wrong, I want my future wife to be so cute she causes traffic accidents, but looks are relative, fleeting, and way less important than what is on the inside.

Ultimately, we'll all end up looking like wrinkly prunes, and it's going to be way more fun to have a cool wrinkly prune next to you than a grumpy used-to-be-hot prune who none of your friends enjoy being around.

Bully Being Bully

I know this might seem shocking, but not everyone in school leads the homecoming parade, is the starting quarterback, or is elected class president. Most of us have a few friends, a certain spot where we eat lunch, a favorite teacher, and at least one kid who bullies us. Bullies are to school what tigers are to the zoo. Outside of school I haven't really dealt with many bullies, much in the same way that outside of the zoo I haven't seen many tigers. Bullies are in every school, and just like overpriced snacks in a vending machine, they aren't going away anytime soon.

It seems like everything is fair game to a bully. I and countless others have been teased about the most stupid and random stuff:

- Being too smart: "What up, Brains McGee"
- Being too "not-smart": "Attention, Mister Poo-for-Brains"
- Being skinny: "Hey, Stick Boy"
- Being fat: "Yo, Tubs"

And you know how the best bad guys in movies are the ones who know how to exploit their opponent's flaws? Bullies are like that, too. ADHD is way more of a blessing than a curse, but it gives people great ammunition if they want to bully you.

Since we are on the topic of tigers, a few years ago a tiger attacked one of his trainers (Roy, of the famous Siegfried and Roy show) during a performance in Las Vegas. The media was in a frenzy, and everyone from Tony the Tiger to *Tiger Beat* magazine had an opinion. The comedian Chris Rock was doing a comedy special on TV around this time and said (loosely), "Man, that tiger didn't go crazy. That tiger went tiger!"

Ever since Chris Rock said that, whenever it comes to bullies all I can think of is, "Man, that bully wasn't being mean. That bully was being bully." Why do people tease and bully others? I don't know. Why does pasta not go well with orange juice? No clue. We could spend the next 300 pages analyzing why some kids must habitually mistreat other kids. Maybe their mom gave them vegetables instead of birthday cake, or they have low self-esteem and need to bring everyone else down to their level, or they have huge egos and need to stroke them. Whatever the reason, it doesn't change the fact that mean words hurt.

It helps to remember that mean words don't have to define you. Just because people tease you about something doesn't mean it's true or that you will be like that forever!*

Besides, usually someone will tease you for being above or below average in pretty much anything, and guess what? Being average is for suckers.

*Anyone can change, even bullies.

Old Ladies and Inappropriate Handshakes Don't Mix

I'm notorious for saying the wrong thing to the wrong person at the wrong time. Perfect example: I used to hang out with this cool old lady who lived down the street and we would rap out about the weather and what our neighborhood was like in earlier years. We were getting to be pretty good buddies and mutually decided we needed something exclusive between us, like a secret handshake. She suggested we interlock fingers or something, and it reminded me of a secret handshake I used to do in middle school where you made your fingers intersect and it was supposed to look like . . . something dirty.

So I was like, "This handshake looks like the ones we used to do back in the day." And she was like, "What handshakes back in the day?"

As a good friend, I didn't want her to feel uninformed, so I showed her. After I explained what it was supposed to look like, she turned really pale and made a gagging noise. The noise she made was so awkward and her face looked so bummed, I really wished we had come up with a different handshake.

This Has Been Another Episode Of:
KNOW YOUR AUDIENCE!

Social Media
FOR
DUMMIES

Sometimes I wish I had a public relations specialist who could help me get out of trouble when I do something without thinking it through. Like if I ate someone's cupcake, my PR specialist would issue the statement, "My client did not mean to eat his friend's pastry. He did see the note 'Shelby' on it, however, he logically assumed that the cupcake's name was Shelby, not that it belonged to his friend Shelby."

Since I don't have a PR specialist, I'm forced to monitor my own actions. In the example above, I had already eaten the cupcake and was just trying to do damage control so that my friend Shelby wouldn't get mad.

Of course, even more effective than doing damage control is avoiding issues before they start. This is especially important when it comes to the Internet. You'd be amazed at how many ADHD brains put stuff out there that will have them doing massive damage control later on. Let's be serious, we've all done something (knowingly or unknowingly) that might be embarrassing, inappropriate, or a little bit against the law. While it's all fun and games to joke about with your friends, one of the stupidest things you can do is post photos all over the

Internet of yourself doing something regrettable. Same with writing something that may come back to haunt you later. If you ever want a job as a firefighter, teacher, politician, police officer, children's book author, or just about anything else, you have to be aware of what you say and post online.

 farcebook

 YOU
I TOTALLY RAGED FOR PAULY'S BIRTHDAY!! THINGS GOT SUPER CRAZY, I MADE OUT WITH A COW...
Sunday at 1:57am · Comment · Like

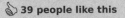 👍 **39 people like this**

 Cow
Jerk!!!!!
Sunday at 2:04am · Like · 👍 *11*

 Pauly Partysauce
We totally did rage!!
Sunday at 2:09am · Like

Aunt Olivia Newton-John
This doesn't sound good. I think your mother and I will have a talk about this...
Sunday at 8:12am · Like

Cute Girlyoulike
Why would you brag about this?
Sunday at 11:25am · Like · 👍 *14*

   Shelby
Dude, did you eat my cupcake?
20 minutes ago · Like · 👍 *1*

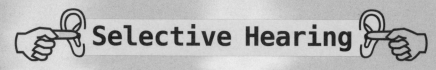
Selective Hearing

I'll be honest, I'm not that good at listening. When someone tells me their name or starts talking longer than five words, I sometimes tune out. Sorry to bum you out if you've introduced yourself to me. But I don't *fully* tune out (more like 70 percent tune out), so I can usually pay attention to the bulk of what a person is saying. Normally this works out fine, and people never really catch on to the fact that I'm not giving them my complete undivided attention. (Now that I think about it, I don't think I've ever had my attention completely undivided for anything.)

Sometimes, though—especially with my parents—it can be a huge problem when I assume they said things they didn't or I make up the fine details in my mind. So, if you tell me not to touch the brownies you made because they are all for your friend's birthday, don't be too upset if I have brownie crumbs all over my mouth because I only remembered you saying, "Make sure not to eat all the brownies I made." (And since I only had a few, I didn't eat *all* of them.)

Good Idea: If you're told something important, consider writing it down or putting it in your calendar or phone so you don't forget it. Also, I've come up with a nice group of phrases to get people to repeat themselves.

- "Sorry, could you say that one more time?"

- "There was a bird over your shoulder distracting me. What was that again?"

- "I was doing a quick visual scan for ninjas, can you repeat that?"

- "Let me make sure I heard you correctly—say it again, please."

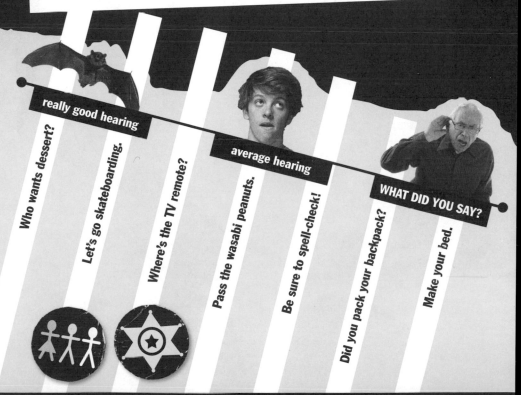

really good hearing

average hearing

WHAT DID YOU SAY?

Who wants dessert?

Let's go skateboarding.

Where's the TV remote?

Pass the wasabi peanuts.

Be sure to spell-check!

Did you pack your backpack?

Make your bed.

Good Point

Most people can't be good at everything. I know very few neurosurgeons playing in the NFL or fashion designers who are experts on Mesozoic history. Most likely you'll discover a few things you are into (like football or fashion) and probably quite a few you aren't (like biology or Mesozoic history). The best advice I've received in regards to life is to put as much time and energy as you can into the classes or activities you love and to try your hardest to suck as little as possible in the things you struggle with.

Side Note: If you feel your talent is bullying, please don't use it on people. Instead of being mean to nerds, outcasts, and nonathletic people, look into a career as a professional wrestler.

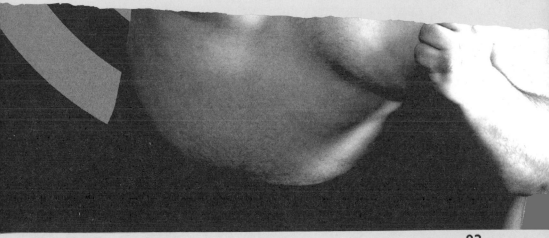

VICTORIES

When I was 17 years old, I had my favorite teacher of all time in U.S. History. And since I loved being American and studying history, that class was a perfect match for my interests, just like ice cream and sugar cones. At a time in my life when the only thing I dominated was a bowl of cereal, it felt really good to bring that same kind of domination to the classroom. Instead of the kid who sucked at math and talked out of turn, I was the smart one who knew all the answers. It was a real confidence booster to know that I could be good at something in school.

The cool thing is, not everyone needs to do well in history to feel better about themselves. My little brother has a brain that is similar to mine and his school had woodshop. Even though he was getting manhandled in English class, he'd get to woodshop and make the most amazing stuff (like a paddle and wooden cross to stab vampires with). It's really empowering to be good at something.

You may suck at public speaking . . .

But you rule at cake decorating!

Real Talk

Why should you care about my U.S. History class? Well, you shouldn't. But you should care about finding a subject or interest that you excel in. Humans like to be praised, and it's important for your self-esteem to have something you feel passionate about. Even if you're not the best at it, having an area or activity that you enjoy is really important. So what if you're not good at certain subjects in school? Don't forget that you're a beast when it comes to [video games/tennis/making pasta/being a beef jerky connoisseur/finger painting/etc.*]!

*Make sure whatever you enjoy doing is legitimate. You may be really good at hunting bald eagles, but you should definitely not do that!

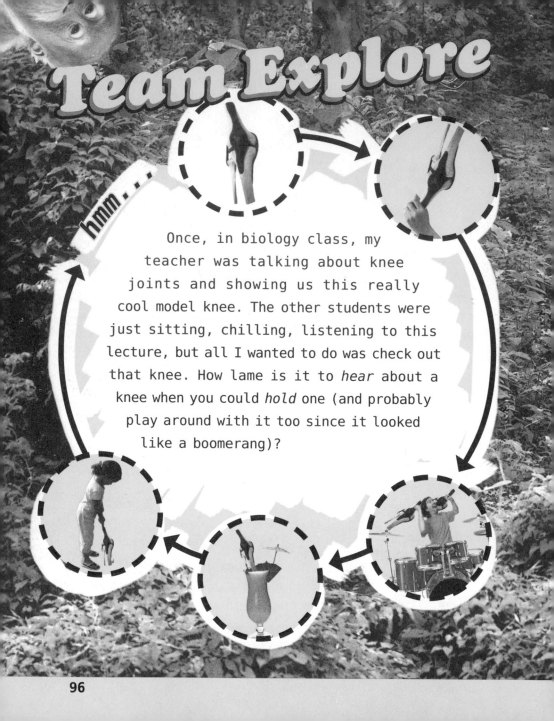

Team Explore

hmm . . .

Once, in biology class, my teacher was talking about knee joints and showing us this really cool model knee. The other students were just sitting, chilling, listening to this lecture, but all I wanted to do was check out that knee. How lame is it to *hear* about a knee when you could *hold* one (and probably play around with it too since it looked like a boomerang)?

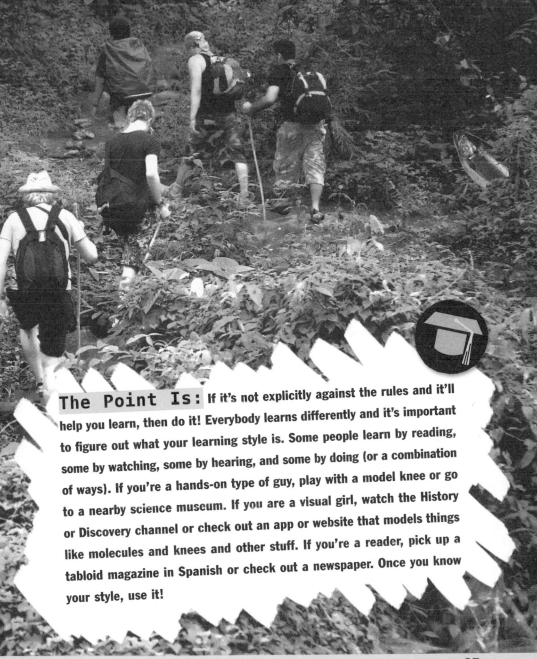

The Point Is: If it's not explicitly against the rules and it'll help you learn, then do it! Everybody learns differently and it's important to figure out what your learning style is. Some people learn by reading, some by watching, some by hearing, and some by doing (or a combination of ways). If you're a hands-on type of guy, play with a model knee or go to a nearby science museum. If you are a visual girl, watch the History or Discovery channel or check out an app or website that models things like molecules and knees and other stuff. If you're a reader, pick up a tabloid magazine in Spanish or check out a newspaper. Once you know your style, use it!

Putting an Assignment on Payment Plans

I can't stand homework assignments that are given months in advance of their due date. Like those assignments you get on the first day of class that are due at the end of the semester and will account for 60 percent of your grade. I don't know about you, but I tend to put things in two categories:

1) Things that need to be done really soon.

2) Things that don't need to be done really soon.

Anything that needs to be done really soon (like eating, filling my car with gas, and surfing) are generally taken care of pretty quickly because they're necessary. I'm all about the necessary. If necessary was a person, necessary and I would sip exotic drinks and have delightful candlelit dinners. Special brains understand necessary, it means we have to do it—no excuses.

Now, if something doesn't have to be done immediately, does that make it not necessary? I *could* do some of next week's homework or go over extra problems . . . but is it necessary right now?

When a teacher announces a huge exam a week in advance, my brain typically says something like this: "My wish for extra playtime got granted! One week means six days not to stress about studying, and one day to stress—right?" And the always lethal: "You should ignore all the previous times this hasn't worked out and just leave everything until the last minute."

Anyway, leaving stuff until the last minute always tends to bite me in the butt (in a metaphorical sense), so I've been working on getting a little bit done in advance. I mean, if you like being bitten in the butt, then I guess you should keep leaving things until the last minute (not that enjoyment of butt bites is a red flag or anything). In all seriousness, life is so much less stressy when you take care of big tasks before they're due.

BREAK IT DOWN

I hate trying to balance a full plate of responsibilities the same way I hate uncooked broccoli and trash juice (you know, the liquid puddle at the bottom of the trash can). Whenever I have multiple important things to do (for example studying for three exams during finals week, getting groceries, and taking the dog for a walk), I might as well have 100 huge things to do. I don't know what it is, but my brain just freaks out over multiple assignments.

Advice: Oh man, I'm so happy to be able to write this book because balancing multiple tasks is one of those skills I had to learn the hard way. A lot of research explains that special brains are a little different from non-special brains—particularly the section of the brain that deals with multitasking. (Special brains are over-developed in the awesomeness section.)

Anyway, here's some really good advice to avoid freaking out when you have to do more than two or three different tasks.

- **PRIORITIZE:** If you have a lot of responsibilities to take care of, ask yourself if anything can be put off until things slow down. Can you wait to get new guitar strings or reschedule a haircut until after midterms? Sometimes you have to cancel plans or say no.

- **MAKE A LIST:** Compile a list of stuff you have to do before you head out so you're not making adjustments on the fly. Nothing is worse than being somewhere and realizing that your next errand was five minutes from where you were just two errands before. Factor in traffic (if appropriate), location, importance (knock off the big ones first if you can), and the amount of stress each task entails.

- **KEEP CALM:** Having more than one thing to study or do for the day can feel overwhelming. Try to free up as much of the day as possible (in case things take longer than expected). Wake up early and start chipping away at your first task, then go onto the second task, etc. If you're making progress, you'll feel less stressed. It's like when I have to eat something gross, like Brussels sprouts. Just get started and keep eating one bite after the other, and don't stop or get distracted until everything on the plate is gone.

- **EATING AND EXERCISE:** Don't think that being under deadline is an excuse to let your eating and exercising habits slip. You may save 10 minutes by getting a burger and soda at some fast-food place, but you just gave your body grease and processed crap for fuel—bad fuel means bad performance. Also, be sure to do something physical every few hours. A quick power lap around the library keeps your endorphins moving after being deep in a book for an hour. Just be careful that your power lap around the library doesn't turn into a two-hour distraction after passing through the magazine section.

NOTE TO SELF:

Consider a helper monkey to aid in multitasking responsibilities . . .

Lazy?

A lot of people have misinterpreted me as lazy (and still do). I was so slow in the morning getting ready for school, I would have been okay with showing up to first period in my pajamas wrapped up in a blanket. Same thing with homework: molasses dripping down a wall of sandpaper was probably faster than me getting started on an assignment.

Those examples don't mean I'm lazy, though. They just mean I have a tough time focusing on things that don't really interest me. When something interests me, I am pretty much the opposite of lazy. When we started studying mobsters and all this other cool prohibition era stuff, I used to spend hours reading about Al Capone, Bugsy Siegel, and all these other cool guys. When I started writing this book, I used to spend whole days writing. I blew off surfing with friends, meeting people for lunch, and other stuff just to write.

I know a lot of special-brained friends who mistakenly get called out as lazy. If you're lazy, then you're lazy . . . but don't buy into the hype when haters mistake your disinterest for laziness.

Worrying

Some days my brain can spend the entire day concerned about all the things I have to do. You know what I realized? If worrying about getting work done was an actual job, I could probably lock down an employee of the month award at least two months a year. My brain would rather freak out about all the work it has to do than sit down and get it done.

Real Talk: I've never climbed Mount Everest, but I have a feeling you wouldn't get very far if you stood at the foot of the mountain and freaked out about how you were going to do it. A better strategy is to start at the bottom and take one step after the other until you arrive at the top.* Same thing with worrying: If you sit back and stare at whatever task is freaking you out, you'll spend the entire day shell-shocked. Just step up to that challenge and take it one step at a time!

*Important: If you are going to climb Mount Everest, you should probably look into a little more advice than "one foot after the other."

Could Have Been a Millionaire

Like most of us, every few days I get a really good idea for something. Over the years I've considered everything from opening a meat pie restaurant to breeding purebred pugs. While some of my friends and family might beg to differ, I feel most of my ideas have the potential to be really successful. The problem is, as soon as I start getting serious about something, a new idea pops into my head. One week I want to be a stockbroker, the next week a sailboat racer.

One day my friend gave me some really good advice: "Pick one thing and do it until you either succeed or hit a wall." This is great advice because we special brains tend to leave a bunch of half-finished ideas all around us. Since those ideas are never completed, we never find out if they are successful or not. So pick an idea and stick with it. Even if you get bored, see it through to success or failure . . . and *then* go pick another idea.

FYI

Apart from winning the lottery or finding an oil reserve under your backyard, there aren't many ways to get rich quick without putting in some hard work.

The Hill of Not Followed Through Ideas

FUTURE EMPLOYMENT?

Right now some people are holding down some pretty awesome job titles. Fifty years ago you wouldn't find many professional runners, gossip bloggers, or drift racers. But now it seems like you can make anything into a job if you are good enough at it. Which got me thinking . . .

BUSINESS NE

HELP WANTED

Seeking **professional nicknamer**. Must have 10+ years experience. Firm that is filled with lots of nice, attractive single women seeks professional nicknamer to give us all creative and funny nicknames. Must be able to make at least 5–10 original variations around an employee's name every week. Salary: $300,000/year. 20–30 hours a week. Includes vacation time, flexible hours, and casual corporate workplace. No résumé needed, just stop in and say hi.

Non-Chinese Chinese food connoisseur wanted: Do you enjoy eating Chinese food and then talking about how you just ate Chinese food? Local agency seeks non-Chinese Chinese food taster to try different Chinese food restaurants around town and offer critiques and praises. Qualifications: 1) Must enjoy Chinese food. 2) Must enjoy talking and thinking about Chinese food.

GD

The
duct,
nomi
the p
both
St.
A
plag
nega
quar
C
sect
sect
0.5
T

A FEW REAL-WORLD PEOPLE YOU SHOULD KNOW ABOUT

Thousands of real people have lived (or are living) interesting lives. Everyone is into different stuff, but I'm sure whatever floats your boat, you can find somebody whose life can show you what's possible (whether that person has a special brain or not). Here are three people out of hundreds who I think are cool, but I strongly suggest you find your own.

Theodore "Teddy" Roosevelt. Teddy was a sick child who had to be homeschooled before making his way into Harvard (where he competed in boxing). His love of nature and exercise made him the most adventurous and outdoorsy U.S. president ever. Roosevelt fought in a bunch of wars, had a bunch of different cool jobs (like sheriff and writer), and went on safari in Africa.

Real Talk: As a 50-year-old U.S. president, Roosevelt thought U.S. troops were getting "soft" and demanded that the cavalry be able to ride 100 miles every three days. When the cavalry thought his orders were too difficult, Roosevelt rode 100 miles in one day to prove them wrong.

Richard Branson. There's a lot more to life than making money, like flying around the world in blimps and building space ships! Branson has done all those things and more. He struggled a lot academically when he was younger, but slowly he turned a record business into a multi-billion-dollar group of companies. That's cool and all, but the real reason I think Richard Branson is the man is because he goes on some of the gnarliest adventures all over the world. He dominates at hot air balloon racing and boat racing and recently kite-surfed the English channel (at 60 years old).

Fun Fact:
Richard Branson is busy working on Virgin Galactic, a commercial space travel company!

Abraham Lincoln. I know, two U.S. presidents in a list of three people, but I like Abe Lincoln for totally different reasons from why I like Teddy Roosevelt. Abraham Lincoln was an unlikely president. When he was young, his family considered him lazy and he only had a year and a half of formal education (he never had a high school degree but self-taught himself to become a lawyer). It's cool that one of our most amazing presidents had a business that failed, had horrible luck with the ladies, and overcame some pretty devastating setbacks.

Abe's Boat: A $4.7 billion aircraft carrier is named after him (the USS *Lincoln*).

HERE ARE SEVERAL MORE PEOPLE TO LOOK INTO

Andrew Carnegie, Ellen DeGeneres, Tina Fey, Li-Young Lee, Debbi Fields, Richard Halliburton, Steve Nash, Gloria Estefan, Chuck Norris, Quentin Tarantino, Kurt Warner, and Oprah Winfrey.

RAAA!

Rabid pandadactyl

Video Games vs. a Slap in the Face from Reality

Real life doesn't have a reset button. Most people know that in theory, but very few truly understand that you don't get many second chances. You'd be amazed at how many times we special brains let opportunities pass us by.

Here's a great example of blowing it: A few years back I was cast in the first episode (called the pilot) of a TV show. In the show I played one of the main character's good friends (the main character was Kristen Bell who has been in a bunch of really cool movies). I had a pretty integral role in the first episode and it's possible that I could have become one of the major characters on the show. After the first episode the show got picked up for a season, and to celebrate there was a party at the head producer's mansion overlooking the Sunset Strip. A lot of Hollywood movers-and-shakers and heavy hitters were there.

As I have said, this book is the culmination of things I've learned the hard way, so to make a long story short, I found an energy drink and a bag of licorice that mysteriously had appeared in my car before the party. Let's just say licorice and Red Bull did not help bring about my calmest behavior. I didn't destroy anything or get escorted out, but I was easily the most energetic person there. I thought my behavior was perfect, which it was . . . if I happened to be at a rodeo.

Dang, reset!

I had one chance to make a positive impression with the guy who made the movie *Predator*, and I spent it tripping out on sugar and caffeine. He probably doesn't remember talking to me, but I do, and I didn't bring my A-game. It was a missed opportunity, and at the least, I could have asked if he could set me up on a date with Rachel McAdams.

As special brains, sometimes we forget that you can't control when opportunity knocks. Opportunities are like fishes. There are plenty of small ones, but it's very rare to be in the right place at the right time to reel in a big one.

The Bad Day vs. a Slap in the Face from Reality

We all have bad days. Maybe your parents, your teacher, or your boss yelled at you. Maybe nobody yelled at you, but you tripped over a rock and stubbed your toe, or you ruined your favorite T-shirt in the laundry. You might even be pissed because the zoo doesn't have any job openings for a penguin keeper. Whatever the case, some days just aren't meant to go in the highlight books. That's a bummer, and I feel for you, but I'm over letting the littlest things ruin my day. If the restaurant screws up your order and you consider the day wasted, you need a reality check. Bad days are bad days, but bad days don't mean life is over.

Suck it up!

We Only Eat with *Free-Range* Forks

Lately it seems like a lot of people have been going on TV talking about special diets that can lessen the effects of everything from ADHD to arthritis. You also hear a lot about how you should eat free-range chickens, corn-fed beef, salmon that have been fed organic spinach, blah blah blah.

I'm not going to knock anything that helps people, but it's really tough for me to eat gluten-free, dairy-free, or almost any other type of free (I live in Southern California and almost nothing is free here). I have friends who are gluten-free, and they love it, but I just don't have the cooking skills or bank account to upgrade to organic or gluten-free food all the time. It's pretty hard to raise chickens in an apartment, and if I'm on the road I'm not going to bug the drive-thru teller with questions about whether the cow was corn-fed or grass-fed.

On the real, though, I'm definitely not a fast-food junkie. I think the "Eat-as-healthy-as-you-can-afford-or-make-time-for-diet" is a pretty good option for most people. With the "Eat-as-healthy-as-you-can-afford-or-make-time-for-diet," it's all about doing the best you can: If you're on the road and have to get fast food, choose sub sandwiches instead of burgers and fries. If your drink options are soda or water, choose water.

Here are some other simple and mostly affordable ways to eat more healthy. Baby steps!

- Switch from white to wheat on a sandwich.
- Eat less meat (I know, bummer).
- Eat more fish.
- Take vitamins and fish oil pills (fish oil helps the brain focus and vitamins help your brain stay yoked).
- Eat lots of different fruits and veggies.

If you just got a huge bonus at your job and can buy a steer from a cattle farm, then that's cool, too. And if you get on some new trendy diet and it helps you focus tons, then that's awesome—send me an email about it. But don't expect me to get all riled up promoting some diet that involves threshing your own flour and making your own corn flakes from scratch. Meanwhile, if you keep eating foods that aren't making you feel alert and well-powered throughout the day, then try making some changes until things get better (see "Snack Time" on page 122).

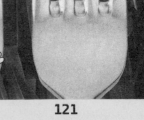

SNACK TIME

YUM!

If I were you, I'd put a sticky note on the top of this page. This page is all about good ideas for snacks, so when you're hungry, all you need to do is find the sticky note and *voilà,* you have a great list of snack ideas.

Snacks are one of those things that reinforce how awesome life can be. Snacks, like puppies and presents, are a pretty good way to cheer yourself up. In fact, a lot of people become obese because they don't know when to put the brakes on snacking. We all know that there are good snacks and bad snacks. Cupcakes are bad snacks: They provide no energy and aren't that healthy. Smoothies are good snacks because they provide solid ingredients and give you enough energy to power out a marathon (or at least run around the block a few times).

Over the years I've worked on perfecting my snack selection to include things that will satisfy my taste buds and provide adequate nutrition. Snacking can be highly creative if you make it that way. If you like bacon in your yogurt, then go for it (just don't expect me to try a bite). You should create your own, but here's my snacking starting lineup.*

*These are my ideas and not a nutritionist-recommended diet!

Basic Snack Staples: Yogurt, beef jerky, cereal bars, peanuts, almonds, pretzels, chewy bars, tortilla chips (with salsa), hummus, apples, oranges, bananas, carrot sticks, cereal, toast, trail mix, soup, oatmeal, edamame, celery . . . you get the picture.

Next-Level Snacking: Grill a seasoned chicken breast, make a smoothie, make guacamole, smoke a sausage, cook pasta, grill a quesadilla, or make a pizza bagel.

Premium Snacking: NY strip steak, Peking duck. Yeah.

More Ideas: Some of these may seem really basic, but when you're hungry you can forget about the simplest things.

- **Super celery:** Celery with peanut butter and pretzel sticks in the grooves.

- **Quesadillicious:** Quesadilla with meat and some green peppers. You can microwave it for a healthier snack or use butter in a frying pan for an indulgence. (For those who don't know what a quesadilla is, it's melted cheese in a folded tortilla.)

- **My power smoothie:** Banana, vanilla almond milk, protein powder, ice, apple juice, and a scoop of chunky peanut butter.

- **The gangster wrapper:** A large tortilla, mayo (or hummus if you have it!), lettuce, tomatoes, green peppers, bacon, some cheese, and a few chicken strips from the grocery store deli. Heat everything, then wrap it up.

Smoothies are great because you can be creative with them.

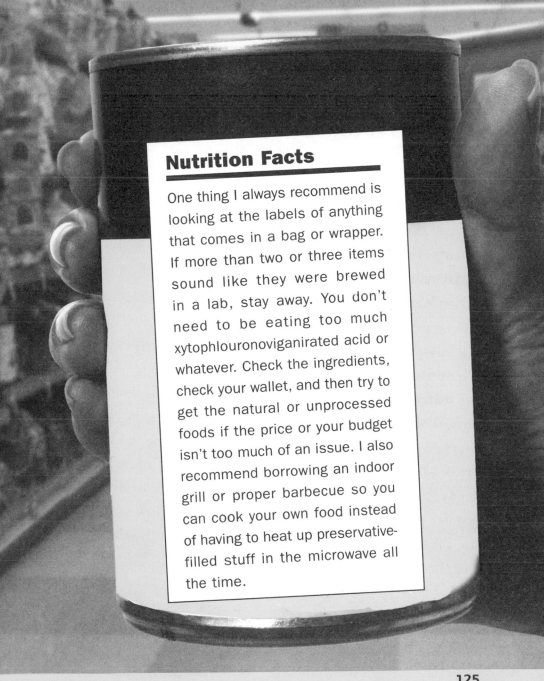

Nutrition Facts

One thing I always recommend is looking at the labels of anything that comes in a bag or wrapper. If more than two or three items sound like they were brewed in a lab, stay away. You don't need to be eating too much xytophlouronoviganirated acid or whatever. Check the ingredients, check your wallet, and then try to get the natural or unprocessed foods if the price or your budget isn't too much of an issue. I also recommend borrowing an indoor grill or proper barbecue so you can cook your own food instead of having to heat up preservative-filled stuff in the microwave all the time.

A Letter to My Ex-Lover, Candy

Dear Candy,

I'm breaking up with you. You've broken my heart too many times and I'm afraid you will never change the way you treat me. Our relationship is unhealthy and I don't have the self-control to enjoy you in moderation. I wish you were healthier and better for me. Sadly, you are not. All the joys we experienced in our encounters were short-lived. You never cared about leaving me lethargic and brain-dead. I always tried to forget how the brief "sugar rush" we would share was inevitably followed by a much longer "Candy coma." You gave me a few minutes of pleasure and left me with a few hours of hurt.

I should have told you sooner, but I've been eating healthier things. I knew this would upset you, so I kept it a secret. It started off with yogurt instead of licorice and steamed carrots instead of hard candy. I've found food that wants the best for me. Wheat crackers have never left me high and dry during sports like you have. While nothing will ever be as sweet as you, I've come to enjoy the rewards associated with eating better. I like thinking clearer and competing longer too much now to love you like I used to. I'm sorry, Candy, but we can't see each other anymore. It's for the best.

Sincerely,

Me

side note

Oh man, my brother just reminded me of the funniest (saddest) story about candy. He has a special brain, too, so our household was candy-free for a reason. All the other kids used to get so excited about Halloween because they would get all this candy. I mean, why else would you think it's cool to dress up like a goblin and ring the doorbells of people you wouldn't dare talk to during the daytime?

But I digress.

Anyway, my parents always made us give away all the candy we collected to the kids at Children's Hospital who were too sick to trick or treat that year. I always thought my parents made us do this to help all the kids who couldn't go out, but my brother just told me that it was because Mom and Dad didn't want to deal with two kids eating a trash bag full of candy on a school night. Apparently, the idea of two sugared-out kids dressed as goblins running around the house till 2:00 a.m. didn't sit well with them.

YUM!

Judge, Jury, and Executioner

This is a book about special brains, ADHD, ninja hamsters, and Chinese food, so why should we bother talking about parents? Well, most of us weren't conceived by spontaneous combustion. Without making you think about an unnecessary visual, don't forget that you are a product of your mom and dad (possibly some slow jams, too). In addition to inheriting the way you look, you probably inherited your special brain as well.

Most scientists agree that ADHD is highly genetic. Some stats say there is an almost 60 percent chance that a parent with ADHD will pass on ADHD to his or her kids. I'm not much of a gambler, but I'd bet money that any rugrats I create will be quite hyperactive. Anyway, the fact that ADHD is often inherited can actually be really useful. I remember how stoked I was to find out that when my dad was younger, he was a special brain, too (I think he still is, but just $1/10$ as much as me). I felt like I finally had someone in the house who understood how frustrating homework or focusing could be. Even though my dad still made me do my homework and punished me for being inappropriate, at least we had a special brain common bond.

Do This: Show your mom or dad a little bit of this book and ask if it resonates at all. Having a mom or dad who can empathize with some of the struggles of a special brain can really help your relationship. Even if you're adopted or not living with your birth parents, you can still get some value out of comparing experiences with the adults in your life.

TIME OUT!

I hate arguing. Arguing is different from debating, which is fun. They make movies about debate teams that feature Laurence Fishburne. Arguing involves emotions and can lead to throwing a dinner plate out the window. Whenever I get into an argument with someone, it's almost impossible for my emotions not to get involved. Emotions mess with my thoughts, and I have a difficult enough time managing my thoughts when I'm not upset.

When you have a heated disagreement with your parents or your significant other, you usually don't debate. You argue. It never used to end well whenever I got into an argument. Either my brain didn't censor anything, causing me to say the most gnarly, mean, unspeakable things, or I couldn't piece together something coherent and would just whimper and whine.

If you notice, I said that my arguments *used* to end like this. The last few years I've worked on incorporating a time-out into the mix.

The time-out strategy came to me one day while watching a Lakers basketball game. It was tied, 30 seconds left, and all the key players were almost fouled out. The game was critical. Emotions and stress were running high. Coach Phil Jackson called a time-out and brought all the players in to discuss strategy. Just being able to walk away from the action for a moment allowed the players to calm their nerves and refocus on the game plan.

As I was watching that game, it dawned on me: "Why don't I incorporate the time-out when I'm in an argument and things get really heated?" It definitely couldn't hurt my efforts to win more arguments and not say regrettable things.

A few days later I got into an argument with my mom about something stupid (I was probably angry because my brother ate my sandwich or something), and the argument was snowballing into a really intense confrontation. My special brain was going a million miles a minute, and then I remembered to blow the whistle and take a time-out: "Mom, I can't gather my thoughts really well, and before I say something really mean, I'm going to take a time-out and go in my room to gather my thoughts. Can we please reconvene this discussion in a few minutes?"

I can't remember if I won or lost the argument, but I know the time-out helped me make my point better when I came back.

I strongly advise incorporating a time-out when arguments get intense with your parents, a boyfriend or girlfriend, your boss, a sibling, or a crazy person.

Following Your Heart

A few days ago I was thinking deep thoughts (like about taming a man-eating lion or something) when I started thinking about my experience with college. In this book I'm sharing some of the things I've learned, and it's always helpful to hear people's advice, but sometimes advice shouldn't be followed. For me, I wish I didn't follow the advice to go to college at 18.

When I was 18 I really wanted to take a break from school. I loved learning, but I had this feeling in my heart that I needed to get some things figured out. The extended family members and authority figures I talked to thought it would be okay to take some time off. But my parents didn't agree. They were concerned that if I took a break before going to college, it would be highly unlikely that I would eventually go.

My options were: If I chose college, my life would have been very cushy (I was fortunate to have money saved for my tuition), and if I chose not to go to college, my life would have been pretty difficult (I would have had my parents' love, yet no financial support). Ultimately, I ignored my gut instinct, chose the safe path, and went to a school in Los Angeles.

Hey, listen up!

When I showed up on campus, I realized it was a huge mistake. My heart had been right, and I wasn't ready to deal with the college social, academic, or living scene. I didn't know what I wanted to study, I didn't know how to relate to the other students, and all I really knew was that I didn't want to be there. I didn't cut my hair for the entire year and I became a hermit in my dorm room when I wasn't out surfing. It was the most anti-social and awkward period of my life. I literally hated school and was academically indifferent. My grades got crushed, and by the time I started to pull myself out of my slump, it was too late to get into any major I was interested in because my GPA was so bad.

If I could rewind time I would have told myself to be tough and take the difficult path. Having the financial help to get a college degree was an amazing gift, and I still feel guilty and regret that I wasted it. Sure, it would have been difficult to support myself fresh out of high school, but I have a feeling I would have been eager to go to college once I was ready and knew what to study. I include this story to demonstrate that sometimes the regret that comes with taking an easy path is much harder to swallow than the risks of choosing the more difficult path.

But there's more to the story! If I hadn't gone to school, I wouldn't have been in Los Angeles, which wouldn't have brought me into acting. Acting gave me plenty of free time and spare change—which bought lots of plane tickets to surf all over the world—which was pretty awesome. Plus, I learned a lot about life and myself in those four years, which allowed me to write this book. So on the flip side, something good came out of something really bad.

I know it sounds cliché, but if you make a bad choice, like me, life goes on—and you never know what awesomeness may come out of your alternate path.

Big DREAMS

We special brains like to dream big. Big dreams require big commitments. The problem with following your dream is that there's no guarantee it will come true. It's not like God or some higher being delivers the goods on everything you ask for. Chasing big dreams can lead to big failures. If you set out to become an ice-cream chef, there are a few possible outcomes:

1) Your special brain creates the most mind-blowing flavors ever, your ice cream becomes a global sensation, and you become rich enough to buy an island.

2) You waste a lot of time, money, and effort in an ice-cream dream that doesn't take off. You're in debt for a long time and your ego feels like Mike Tyson punched it.

3) You end up somewhere in the middle. Maybe your ice-cream creations make enough money to keep the lights on, or you didn't do so well but learned a lot from your mistakes.

Following Your Dreams!

Guaranteed Results*

*Results totally not guaranteed. You could also fail miserably. But you have to try to find out.

This book isn't meant to be a fairy tale, and I'm not going to tell you that your idea for a golf cart—mounted yogurt machine is a guaranteed success. The reality is that most small businesses fail, and most dreams don't come true.

BUT!!!!!!!

Somebody has to be the next great ice-cream chef, and you have just as much right to be that chef as anyone else. Not only that, but if you never pursue your dreams you'll never know if you could have been one of the few people to succeed in making it happen.

(So go for it!)

Glossary

ADHD: Attention deficit hyperactivity disorder. People with ADHD have differences in the parts of their brains that control attention and activity. ADHD used to be called ADD, attention deficit disorder, but it's officially called ADHD now. There are three types:

- Hyperactive type: People with this type often fidget, squirm, and find it hard to sit still or be quiet. They might talk a lot, and sometimes when they shouldn't (like interrupting others or during a quiet time at school). They have lots of energy.

- Inattentive type: For people with this type, it's hard to focus. They might have trouble finishing things they start or get easily distracted. They might forget things, lose things, and have trouble following directions.

- Combined type: These people have traits from both types.

Hater: Someone who reacts negatively to you. The opposite of someone offering some love (approval or good feelings) is to offer some "hate" (criticism or negative feelings), thus making him or her a hater.

Janky: In reference to an inanimate object, it means poorly made or dilapidated. In reference to a person or action, it refers to something being busted up, or just "not good."

Meds: Prescription medicine prescribed by a licensed doctor. The most common are Ritalin, Adderall, and Strattera. Ritalin and Adderall are stimulants that affect the part of the brain that deals with dopamine and norepinephrine. Strattera is a non-stimulant that affects the same part of the brain without being a stimulant (so if you're not good with coffee, or Ritalin and Adderall didn't work, then it might be a good option). Other meds are available that work in different ways to help with ADHD. Talk to your doctor, ask lots of questions, and make sure you're comfortable with the decisions you come to.

Rad: Short for radical. Another way of saying: awesome, cool, amazing, or good. Can be attributed to people, places, and things.

Slow jams: Love songs. See Luther Vandross or Marvin Gaye. Also known as music that talks about love and encourages people to make babies.

Stoked: Really excited. Like, really, really excited! Like, you're so excited, you're not just excited . . . you're stoked! You can be stoked on ideas, the weather, a song, or nothing (and just be stoked on life).

Index

A

Adderall, 139
ADHD
  famous people with, 78–79
  genetics, 128–129
  telling people about, 12–13
  types of, 138
  using as excuse, 16–17
  See also Special brains
Adults
  appropriate behaviors with,
    86–87
  making friends with,
    72–73, 74–75, 86–87
  See also Authority figures
AKIR syndrome, *See*
    Automatically Keeping
    It Real (AKIR)
    syndrome
American sign language
    (ASL), 25
Anger, time-out strategy for,
    130–131
Arguing, 130–131
Assumptions, danger of, 34–35
Authority figures
  ADHD as excuse for
    behavior, 16–17
  asking for help from, 33
  comparing ADHD
    experiences with,
    128–129
  dealing with haters, 12–13
  dolphin versus elephant
    brains, 6–7
  learning from, 74–75
  making friends with,
    72–73, 74–75
  psychiatrists/doctors, 4,
    56–57, 139
  rules, understanding,
    50–51
  selective hearing with,
    90–91
  tasks, clarifying with,
    34–35
  time-out strategy with,
    130–131

"You do you, I'll do me"
    strategy, 14–15
Automatically Keeping It Real
    (AKIR) syndrome, 19

B

Bad days, dealing with,
    118–119
Behavior
  ADHD as excuse for, 16–17
  keeping it real, 18–19
  managing unacceptable
    behavior, 10–11, 86–87
  observant behavior, 58–59
  tapping and twirling, 71
Bell, Kristen, 116
Brains, *See* Special brains
Branson, Richard, 78, 113
Bullying, 82–85, 93

C

Candy, 126–127
Choices, making
  following your heart,
    132–135
  foods, 120–125
Chores, 34–35
Christie, Agatha, 78
Classroom seating, 62–63
College
  assignments, 26–27
  attending, 73, 132–133
  course requirements, 25
  SAT accommodations, 31
Compliments, giving, 18–19
Conversations
  asking for repetition, 91
  listening skills, 9, 90–91
  turn taking, 8–9
  when to be quiet, 20–21
Criticism
  giving, 18–19
  taking, 44–45

D

Dating, 76–77, 80–81
Decision making
  following your heart,
    132–135
  sticking up for personal
    decisions, 14–15

Diet and nutrition, *See* Food
Disguises, assuming, 10–11
Distractibility, *See* Focusing
Distractions
  classroom seating and,
    62–63
  following through, 108–109
  homework and, 29
  Internet, 21
  need for quiet, 20–21, 72
  racing brain, 54–55
  removing, 52–53
  television, 42–43
  test taking and, 30–31
  tornados, 63
  See also Focusing
Doctors, 4, 56–57, 139
Dreams, pursuing, 136–137

E

Eating healthy, *See* Food
Einstein, Albert, 78
Emotions
  arguing and time-out
    strategy, 130–131
  overreacting, 46–47
Employment, *See* Jobs
Excuses, 16–17
Exercising
  for maintaining focus, 67,
    102
  tapping and twirling
    strategies, 71
Expectations, asking for
    specifics about, 34–35

F

Failure, fear of, 46–47
Families, *See* Parents/families
Famous people
  with ADHD, 78–79
  as role models, 9, 112–113
Fidgeting in class, 70–71
Fish oil pills, 121
Focusing
  disinterest and, 105
  following through, 108–109
  inattentiveness
    characteristics, 138
  need for quiet, 20–21, 72

removing distractions,
52–53
in school, 62–63, 66–67
during tests, 30–31
tips for, 67, 121
See also Distractions
Following through, 108–109
Food
effects on focusing and
learning, 67
healthy eating, 102,
120–121, 125
snacks, 122–124
sugar and candy, 126–127
Foot tapping, 70–71
Freaking out, 46–47
Fresh Prince of Bel-Air, The, 62
Friends
adults as, 72–73, 74–75,
86–87
finding common interests
with, 6–7
help from in class, 67
social media, 88–89
"you do you, I'll do me"
strategy, 14–15
See also Social life
Future
dealing with bad days,
118–119
fear of failure, 46–47
finding interests and
talents, 92–93
following your heart,
132–135
growing old, 80–81
jobs, 48–49, 110–111
making choices, 132–135
pursuing dreams, 136–137
responsible Internet use,
88–89
role models, 78–79,
112–115
taking advantage of
opportunities, 116–117

G

Games, foot tapping, 71
Genetics, 128–129

H

Halloween, 127
Haters
dealing with, 12–13, 33,
105
defined, 138
Health care professionals, 4,
56–57, 139
Hearing, selective, 90–91
Help, asking for, 32–33
Homework
modifying assignments,
26–27
procrastination, 98–99
tips for, 28–29
Hyperactivity
characteristics of, 6–7, 138
fidgeting in class, 70–71
racing brain, 54–55
strategies for dealing with,
10–11
See also Distractions;
Focusing

I

Inattentiveness
characteristics of, 10, 138
See also Distractions;
Focusing
Interests
finding common interests,
6–7
focusing on talents, 92–93,
94–95
following through with
ideas, 108–109
following your heart,
132–135
laziness versus disinterest,
104–105
occupations and, 48–49,
110–111
Internet
distractions on, 21
social media, 88–89

J/L

Jackson, Phil, 130
Jobs, 48–49, 110–111
Laziness, 104–105
Learning strategies
asking for help, 32–33
differences in, 32–33

finding your learning style,
96–97
focusing in class, 66–67
making topics interesting,
60–61
need for more time to learn,
64–65
See also School
Lincoln, Abraham, 114
Listening skills
in conversation, 9
selective hearing, 90–91
Lists, making, 101
Looks, paying attention to,
80–81

M/N

Maintenance men, 71
Mean words, *See* Bullying;
Haters
Medications
caution about, 4
discussing with your doctor,
56–57
effect on focusing and
learning, 55, 67
types of, 139
Multitasking, 100–103
Neeleman, David, 79
Negative feedback, *See*
Criticism
Notes, borrowing, 67
Nutrition, *See* Food

O

Observant behavior, 58–59
Occupations, 48–49, 110–111
Old people, making friends
with, 74–75, 86–87
Opportunities, taking
advantage of, 116–117
Orfalea, Paul, 79
Overreacting, 46–47

P

Parents/families
arguing and time-out
strategy, 130–131
comparing ADHD
experiences with,
128–129
selective hearing with,
90–91
See also Authority figures

Pediatricians, 57
Photos, posting on Internet, 88–89
Physical activity, *See* Exercising
Positives, focusing on, 44–45, 76–77
Prioritizing responsibilities, 101
Procrastination, 98–99
Professional wrestlers, 93
Psychiatrists, 56–57
Put-downs, *See* Bullying; Haters

Q/R

Quiet, need for, 20–21, 72
Rapid foot tapping (RFT), 70–71
Ritalin, 139
Rock, Chris, 84
Role models, 9, 78–79, 112–115
Roosevelt, Theodore, 112
Rules, understanding, 50–51

S

SAT, extended time for, 30–31
School
    bullying, 82–85
    classroom seating, 62–63
    cutting class, 72–73
    dolphin versus elephant brains, 6–7
    failing a subject, 38–39
    fidgeting in class, 70–71
    finding your learning style, 96–97
    focusing in class, 20–21, 66–67
    grades, 36–39, 44–45
    homework, 28–29, 98–99
    laziness versus disinterest, 104–105
    making friends with adults, 72–73
    making topics interesting, 60–61
    modifying assignments, 26–27
    multitasking and prioritizing, 100–103
    need for more time to learn, 64–65

positive things about, 40–41
struggles with, 22–23
subject areas, 24–25, 36–39, 61, 94–95
talents, finding and focusing on, 92–93, 94–95
teacher attitudes, 22–23
test taking, 30–31, 68–69
worrying about, 106–107
See also Learning strategies
School nurses, 71
Science courses, 25, 61
Secret handshake, 86
Selective hearing, 90–91
Self-esteem, 95
Siegfried and Roy, 84
Sign language, 25
Simon game, 71
Sleeping, 76
Smith, Will, 62
Smoothies, 124
Snacks, 122–124
Social life
    appropriate behaviors with adults, 10–11, 86–87
    bullying, 82–85
    conversations, 8–9
    criticizing and complimenting, 18–19
    dating, 76–77, 80–81
    dealing with haters, 12–13
    finding common interests, 6–7
    making friends with adults, 72–73, 74–75
    social media, 88–89
    taking rejection personally, 44–45
    time-out strategy, 130–131
    "You do you, I'll do me," 14–15
Social media, 88–89
Special brains
    definition and characteristics of, xiii
    dolphins versus elephants, 6–7
    famous people with, 78–79
    multitasking and prioritizing, 100–103

observant nature of, 58–59
racing nature of, 54–55
See also ADHD
Strattera, 139
Sugar, 67, 126–127

T

Talents, finding and focusing on, 92–93, 94–95
Tapping and twirling behavior, 71
Tasks, clarifying, 34–35
Teachers
    asking for help from, 33
    attitudes toward special brains, 22–23
    making friends with, 72
    See also Authority figures
Teasing, 82–85
Television, 42–43
Test taking
    distractions, 30–31
    double-checking answers, 68–69
    extended time for, 30–31
Thomas, Dave, 79
Tigers, 84
Timberlake, Justin, 79
Time-out strategy, 130–131
Tornados, 63
Tutoring services, 29
Twirling pencils, 71
Tyler, Liv, 79

U/V

Unacceptable behavior, avoiding, 10–11, 86–87
USS *Lincoln,* 114
Vitamins, 121

W/Y

Washington, Denzel, 9
Worrying, 46–47, 106–107
"You do you, I'll do me" strategy, 14–15

Photo Credits

Cover, (anatomy dummy) © Arcady31 | Dreamstime.com; (eyeball, used throughout book) © Billyhoiler3 | Dreamstime.com; (orangutan) © Tomonishi | Dreamstime.com; (tacos) © Teamcrucillo | Dreamstime.com; (alien face) © Tihis | Dreamstime.com; (banana) © Paulfairbrother | Dreamstime.com; (surfer) © istockphoto.com/schutzphoto; (Mexican wrestler) © istockphoto.com/ sumnersgraphicsinc • **interior,** all author photos courtesy of Jonathan Chesner • **Pages xi & 12,** (brain, used throughout book) © Mopic | Dreamstime.com; (sunglasses) © Renata2k | Dreamstime.com • **Page xii,** (anatomy dummy) © Arcady31 | Dreamstime.com; (eyeball) © Billyhoiler3 | Dreamstime.com • **Pages xiv–5,** (anatomy dummy) © Arcady31 | Dreamstime.com; (eyeball) © Billyhoiler3 | Dreamstime.com; (flames) © Klikk | Dreamstime.com • **Pages 6–7,** (elephant) © istockphoto.com/GlobalP; (dolphin, repeated throughout book) © istockphoto.com/FourOaks; (kangaroo) © Mato750 | Dreamstime.com • **Pages 8–9,** (boat dashboard) © Vukvuk | Dreamstime.com; (crown emblem) © Dl1on | Dreamstime.com • **Pages 10–11,** (beard & moustache illustrations) © istockphoto.com/Transfuchsian; (trench-coat) © istockphoto.com/emyerson; (fedora) © Rambleon | Dreamstime.com • **Page 13,** (drill sergeant) © istockphoto.com/MTMCOINS • **Pages 14–15,** (sorry face) © Yayayoy | Dreamstime.com; (honey jar) © Antonprado | Dreamstime.com; (honeycomb) © istockphoto.com/Ralf Hettler • **Pages 16–17,** (chicken nuggets 1) © Rimglow | Dreamstime.com, (chicken nuggets 2) © istockphoto.com/amesmcq24; (sauce) © MorganOliver | Dreamstime.com; (police officer) © istockphoto.com/Paul Kline • **Pages 18–19,** (cringing guy) © istockphoto.com/jlmatt; (bodybuilder) © Soleilc | Dreamstime.com; (sorry note) © istockphoto.com/the4js • **Pages 20–21,** (lion) © Epphoto | Dreamstime.com; (boxing gloves) © Brent Hathaway | Dreamstime.com • **Pages 22–23,** (brick wall) © Lichaoshu | Dreamstime.com; (brain splat) © istockphoto.com/T-Immagini • **Pages 24–25,** (galaxy, used throughout book) © Thanunkorn | Dreamstime.com • **Pages 26–27,** (comic illustration TL) © istockphoto.com/apartment; (comic illustrations BL, TR) © istockphoto.com/jpa1999; (face tattoo) © istockphoto.com/pated • **Pages 28–29,** (cringing guy) © Djma | Dreamstime.com; (wedding cake) © Ivonnewierink | Dreamstime.com; (books on cake) © Xuanmai2009 | Dreamstime.com • **Pages 30–31,** (desert road) © Alptraum | Dreamstime.com; (tumbleweed) © Eutoch | Dreamstime.com; (syringe) © Nero67 | Dreamstime.com; (chicken pox) © Justmeyo | Dreamstime.com; (knight) © Demid | Dreamstime.com; (tent village) © Jackf | Dreamstime.com • **Pages 32–33,** (chihuahua L) © Innocent | Dreamstime.com; (Great Dane & chihuahua R) © Isselee | Dreamstime.com • **Pages 34–35,** (zebra pattern) © Seamless | Dreamstime.com; (zebra butt) © Stepanjezek | Dreamstime.com • **Pages 36–37,** (grim reaper) © istockphoto.com/Bliznetsov; (girl) © istockphoto.com/katalinamas; (Jonathan Chesner) • **Pages 38–39,** (classroom) © Monkeybusinessimages | Dreamstime.com; (tombstone) © Martyhaas | Dreamstime.com; (soil) © Stramyk | Dreamstime.com; (coffin) © Snaprender | Dreamstime.com • **Pages 40–41,** (paper & ink) © Allx | Dreamstime.com; (wagon trail) © Philcold | Dreamstime.com • **Pages 42–43,** (TV screen) © Mabelsound | Dreamstime.com; (doily) © Nruboc | Dreamstime.com; (wallpaper) © Monika3stepsahead | Dreamstime.com; (old TV) © Drx | Dreamstime.com; (floral chair) © Mandj98 | Dreamstime.com • **Pages 44–45,** (sand) © Bombaert | Dreamstime.com; (brain) © Mopic | Dreamstime.com; (dolphin) © istockphoto.com/mschalke; (smoothie) © Shebeko | Dreamstime.com; (body) © istockphoto.com/Neustockimages • **Pages 46–47,** (piranha) © istockphoto.com/foodandwinephotography; (faces illustration) © istockphoto.com/mixformdesign • **Pages 48–49,** (dive helmet) © istockphoto.com/ ultramarinfoto; (chef hat) © Plasticrobot | Dreamstime.com; (police hat) © Dcwcreations | Dreamstime.com; (graduation cap) © Vladimir Mucibabic | Dreamstime.com; (camera) © Edwardgerges | Dreamstime.com; (glasses) © Sbc2758 | Dreamstime.com; (beret) © Penywise | Dreamstime.com • **Pages 50–51,** (powdered wig) © istockphoto.com/ph2212; (crocodiles) © Kavram | Dreamstime.com; (wrecked car) © Ib2loud | Dreamstime.com; (monster truck) © Mishella | Dreamstime.com; (car) © Mlan61 | Dreamstime.com; (running man) © Ljupco | Dreamstime.com; (running woman) © istockphoto.com/ powerofforever • **Pages 52–53,** (fern buds) © Wong Hock Weng John | Dreamstime.com; (fern) © Hpphoto | Dreamstime.com; (head-plate) © Kvkirillov | Dreamstime.com; (energy drink) © istockphoto.com/craftvision • **Pages 54–55,** (watch) © Ijansempoi | Dreamstime.com; (bear) © Rwharr | Dreamstime.com; (fishing rod) © Vladvitek | Dreamstime.com; (boat) © Goce | Dreamstime.com; (sandwich) © Klikk | Dreamstime.com; (basket) © Brookebecker | Dreamstime.com; (armpit guy) © Chisnikov | Dreamstime.com • **Pages 56–57,** (doctor) © Avava | Dreamstime.com; (leather texture) © Kutt Niinepuu | Dreamstime.com; (couch) © Mishoo | Dreamstime.com • **Pages 58–59,** (lifeguard) © istockphoto.com/aabejon; (Jonathan Chesner) • **Pages 60–61,** (curling) © istockphoto. com/4FR • **Pages 62–63,** (tornado) © Solarseven | Dreamstime.com; (ants close-up) © Aetmeister | Dreamstime.com; (ants background) © Toxawww | Dreamstime.com; (cheering fan) © Danp68 | Dreamstime.com; (classroom) © istockphoto.com/1001nights; (football player) © Petesaloutos | Dreamstime.com • **Pages 64–65,** (teacher) © Tiero | Dreamstime.com; (chameleon) © Mlipowski | Dreamstime.com; (remote) © Vzion | Dreamtime.com • **Pages 66–67,** (calligraphy) © Frogtravel | Dreamstime.com; (scantron test) © Keith Bell | Dreamstime.com; (bamboo) © Bradcalkins | Dreamstime.com; (fortune cookie) © Demarco | Dreamstime.com • **Page 71,** (foot) © Blueee | Dreamstime.com; (shoe) © istockphoto.com/yellowsarah • **Pages 72–73,** (tile background) © Paulmaguire | Dreamstime.com; (sandwich) © Valentyn75 | Dreamstime.com; (restroom sign) © Medveh | Dreamstime.com; (desk) © Atlasphoto | Dreamstime.com; (locker) © Cenorman | Dreamstime.com; (nurse) © Cybernesco | Dreamstime.com • **Pages 74–75,** (old man) © Creatista | Dreamstime.com; (old woman) © Savannah1969 | Dreamstime.com; (bingo card) © Webking | Dreamstime.com; (poodles) © Darak77 | Dreamstime.com; (rearview mirror) © istockphoto.com/claudio.arnese; (weiner dog) © istockphoto.com/Antagain • **Page 81,** (prunes) © Angelsimon | Dreamstime.com • **Page 83,** (girl) © Stab | Dreamstime.com • **Page 84,** (tiger) © istockphoto.com/domi8nic • **Pages 86–87,** (needle & thread) © Nomadsoul1 | Dreamstime.com; (game show host) © istockphoto.com/LeggNet • **Page 89,** (cow) © Kurt | Dreamstime.com; (toddler) © Emeraldraindropsphotography | Dreamstime.com; (woman on tractor) © Leobruce | Dreamstime.com; (girl) © Katseyephoto | Dreamstime.com; (cupcake) © Stevemcsweeny | Dreamstime.com • **Pages 90–91,** (sound waves) © Cornelius20 | Dreamstime.com; (cake) © Viktorfischer | Dreamstime.com; (bat) © Kirsanovv | Dreamstime.com; (boy) © istockphoto.com/drbimages; (old man) © Mcininch | Dreamstime.com • **Pages 92–93,** (holding football) © Kennethman | Dreamstime.com; (holding paintbrush) © istockphoto.com/ Merzavka; (wrestler) © istockphoto.com/sumnersgraphicsinc • **Pages 94–95,** (fireworks) © Carlosphotos | Dreamstime.com; (chimp) © istockphoto.com/ RichVintage; (skull) © istockphoto.com/FrankCangclooi • **Pages 96–97,** (hiking scene) © Neotakezo | Dreamstime.com; (knee model) © Jennyt | Dreamstime. com; (hand) © Urfingus | Dreamstime.com; (drummer) © Rolmat | Dreamstime.com; (cocktail) © Elenathewise | Dreamstime.com; (golfer) © Rmarmion | Dreamstime.com • **Pages 96–97,** (water) © Catalinus | Dreamstime.com; (boy on tube) © istockphoto.com/kali9; (shark) © Ancello | Dreamstime.com • **Page 101,** (dumbbell) © Ispace | Dreamstime.com • **Page 103,** (toy monkey) © Davinci | Dreamstime.com • **Pages 104–105,** (sloth) © Hotshotsworldwide | Dreamstime.com; (snail) © istockphoto.com/domdeen • **Page 107,** (Mount Everest) © William Fawcett fotoVoyager.com; (mountain goat) © Toddtaulman | Dreamstime.com • **Pages 108–109,** (quarter) © Atustudio | Dreamstime.com; (dollar bills) © Arielmartin | Dreamstime.com; (sailboat) © Digerati | Dreamstime.com; (DJ) © Goce | Dreamstime.com; (pugs) © S-dmit | Dreamstime.com; (martial artist) © Umegass | Dreamstime.com; (meat pie) © Robynmac | Dreamstime.com • **Pages 110–111,** (race car) © Shariffc | Dreamstime.com; (newspaper) © istockphoto.com/DNY59 • **Pages 112–115,** (old book background) © Clintcearley | Dreamstime.com; (picture frames) © istockphoto.com/mxtama; (Theodore Roosevelt) Library of Congress Prints and Photographs Division Washington, D.C. 20540 USA; (spaceship) © Marciomauro | Dreamstime.com; (Abraham Lincoln) Library of Congress Prints and Photographs Division Washington, D.C. 20540 USA (USS *Lincoln*) © Blueice69caddy | Dreamstime.com • **Page 116,** (licorice) © Iperl | Dreamstime.com • **Pages 118–119,** (penguin) © Javarman | Dreamstime.com; (hand) © Koszivu | Dreamstime.com • **Pages 120–121,** (cornfield) © Teresaterra | Dreamstime.com; (fork) © Pioneer111 | Dreamstime.com • **Page 123,** (yogurt parfait) © wando studios inc; (pistachios) © Norman Chan | Dreamstime.com; (orange slice) © istockphoto.com/Suzifoo; (peanut butter & smiley jelly) © cmbritcliffe | Dreamstime.com; (chicken breast) © Kelpfish | Dreamstime.com; (avocados) © Horsewoman | Dreamstime.com; (pizza bagel) © Brookebecker | Dreamstime.com; (steak) © Mrcbro2010 | Dreamstime.com • **Pages 123–124,** (walnuts) © Marek Kolankiewicz; (lettuce & tomato) © istockphoto.com/pixitive; (soup can) © Nruboc | Dreamstime.com • **Pages 125–126,** (candy box) © Indianeye | Dreamstime.com; (heart chocolates) © istockphoto.com/itographer; (creepy clowns) © istockphoto.com/quavondo; (doorway) © Ulucceylani | Dreamstime.com • **Pages 128–129,** (DNA model) © Beawolf78 | Dreamstime.com; (orangutans) © istockphoto.com/dawnn; (minivan) © Mlan61 | Dreamstime.com • **Page 131,** (whistle) © Bradcalkins | Dreamstime.com • **Pages 132–133,** (lion) © Agno_agnus | Dreamstime.com • **Pages 134–135,** (Hollywood sign) © Merkuri2 | Dreamstime.com • **Pages 136–137,** (sea & sky) © Roxana González | Dreamstime.com; (diamonds) © Igorkah | Dreamstime.com; (car) © Alexeywp | Dreamstime.com; (jumping man) © istockphoto.com/Neustockimages; (scuba diver) © Frhojdysz | Dreamstime.com

Acknowledgments

I want to thank the following for helping me make this book: God, Shelby Stanger, Jessica Sinshiemer, Eric Braun, Tasha Kenyon, everyone at Free Spirit, Denise, Treens, Krysteens, Jeff Rowe, P-Lo, J-Mo, J-P, Brizzle, Ms. Drago, Chris, the Box, Reebs, Lugo, and Reb-dawg. The following people read the manuscript and gave feedback: Rebecca Kajander, CPNP, MPH; Anne Frisby; Lucia Chen; Alex Ogren; Chantel Charlebois; and Andrew Ferguson. Thanks!

I want to thank in general: My parents, my big little brother, ACB, Nana & Popop, the Scotts, the Leimbachs, the Ahrens, Auntie Cindy, the Koetts, Faye, Carmen, John Balaz, Sarizzle, Sarah Bakhiet, Gary Peritz, Bruce Boston, Diko, OG Denson Crew, John Sundt, J-A & Diesel (816), the Kemps, GT, Mitch's/Pesky/Matuse crew, Jonathan Van Speier, the town of La Jolla, all my amazing friends, and anyone who's ever been nice to me or encouraged me in anything.

Thank you: All the honorable members of our military, firefighters, police, lifeguards, EMTs, and any other first responders. Thank you for your sacrifices!

About the Author

Jonathan Chesner was diagnosed with ADHD at age 9, and since then he has tried to use his special powers for good (like being creative and energized) instead of evil (like getting sent to the principal's office). He started acting at age 18, and appears in national commercials, including a campaign for Jack in the Box that aired during the Super Bowl, and in television shows such as *Veronica Mars* and *Bones.*

Jonathan attended the University of Southern California and furthered his creative pursuits by turning his off-campus apartment into an art studio/art gallery/surfboard shaping room/T-shirt factory. At 22, Jonathan started his own clothing company, NiZ Couture, a T-shirt line for young adults sold at better surf shops and boutiques in Southern California and Japan. Jonathan's art has been shown in numerous art galleries as well as on his surf couture line. Major surf companies like Von Zipper and Future Fins have incorporated his conceptual work, and he is well-known for his unique and humorous collages.

Jonathan grew up in San Diego, California, and lives in Los Angeles.

Also Available from Free Spirit

Fighting Invisible Tigers
Stress Management for Teens (Revised & Updated Third Edition)
by Earl Hipp
Research suggests that adolescents are affected by stress in unique ways that can increase impulsivity and risky behaviors. This book offers proven techniques that teens can use to deal with stressful situations in school, at home, and among friends. For ages 11 & up.
144 pp.; softcover; 2-color; illust.; 6" x 9"

Heart of a Warrior
7 Ancient Secrets to a Great Life
by Jim Langlas
The inspiration for this book comes from the ancient Korean history of the Hwarang—young student-warriors who worked to strengthen their spirits as well as their fighting skills. Seven principles, rooted in the long tradition of Taekwondo and tied to courtesy, integrity, perseverance, self-control, indomitable spirit, community service, and love, are explored through a mix of storytelling from the Hwarang and writings from the author's former students, describing ways in which they've applied these principles to their own lives and inspiring readers to do the same.
160 pp.; softcover; 2-color; 6" x 9"

For pricing information, to place an order, or to request a free catalog, contact:

Free Spirit Publishing Inc.
217 Fifth Avenue North • Suite 200 • Minneapolis, MN 55401-1299
toll-free 800.735.7323 • local 612.338.2068 • fax 612.337.5050
help4kids@freespirit.com • www.freespirit.com